THE Bridal Registry Book

Leah Ingram

CONTEMPORARY BOOKS
A TRIBUNE NEW MEDIA/EDUCATION COMPANY

Library of Congress Cataloging-in-Publication Data

Ingram, Leah.
    The bridal registry book / Leah Ingram.
        p.   cm.
    Includes index.
    ISBN 0-8092-3334-7 (alk. paper)
    1. House furnishings—Purchasing.
  2. Weddings—Planning.   3. Consumer
education.   I. Title.
TX311.I53   1995
645—dc20   95-33966
                                CIP

Cover and interior design by Amy Nathan
Author photo by Sardi Klein

Copyright © 1995 by Leah Ingram
All rights reserved
Published by Contemporary Books, Inc.
Two Prudential Plaza, Chicago, Illinois 60601-6790
Manufactured in the United States of America
International Standard Book Number: 0-8092-3334-7
10   9   8   7   6   5   4   3   2   1

To Bill, my loving husband and first editor of everything I write
To my daughter Jane, whose gestation period was just a bit shorter than this book's

Contents

Acknowledgments

While some might argue that there's great shopping to be had in and around the Ann Arbor area (and some might argue that I'm one heck of a shopper to boot), there was no way that I alone could have possibly found all the stores, catalogs, and companies with bridal registries that ended up in this book. It is because so many of my friends and family members kept an eye out for bridal registry information that I was able to compile such a diverse collection of places offering bridal registries. To all of you, I thank you.

The following people were especially diligent in sending me or telling me about everything they could get their hands on regarding bridal registries: my mother, Judy Ingram; my mother-in-law, Rita Behre; my aunt-in-law, Patricia Colarullo; and my friends and professional colleagues, Leslie Gilbert Elman, Therese Iknoian, Terri Thompson, LoriBeth Landau, and Maria Anton.

I'd also like to extend a special thanks to the engaged and already married readers of the two wedding Internet newsgroups, soc.couples.wedding and alt.wedding, especially the brides and grooms I surveyed about their registry experience. In researching and writing this book, I constantly picked your brains and you never asked anything in return (except for occasional tidbits of advice). I could not have written this book without your help.

In addition, thank you to Denise Marcil, my agent, who believed in this book when many others didn't and who ended up registering at Lands' End, thanks to me. Also, thanks to Alina Storek, Contemporary Books' resident bride and my editor. Being able to bounce registry questions and ideas off you was invaluable in writing this book. I hope you get everything you registered for.

If I've forgotten to thank anyone in particular, I do appreciate your help but have had a momentary lapse of memory. Understand that this acknowledgement is being written days before my daughter's due date and, well, women who are nine-months (and counting) pregnant are notoriously forgetful.

Introduction

Almost as soon as my husband and I got engaged, friends and family started asking us where we planned to register. Now, my husband and I are less-than-conventional people who happened to have lived on our own for years before getting together. Since we thought you could only register at department stores and we had everything we needed to set up a household together, we didn't register. It wasn't until months after we got married that we found out that my husband, the handyman, could have registered at Home Depot and the music fan in both of us could have registered for our favorite CDs at Tower Records.

More and more retail establishments nationwide are waking up to the idea that there are many brides- and grooms-to-be who are in a similar situation—they have all their household needs, so they want their wedding gifts to better reflect their personal interests. Thankfully, stores selling everything from lumber to lingerie to lanterns are rushing to set up registry services, giving the soon-to-be-married a range of registry options.

This book is designed to be your road map for finding the bridal registry (or registries) that best fits your needs. I've included tried-and-true registry stores, such as Macy's and Michael C. Fina, as well as establishments that are off the beaten registry track, like Tower Records and travel agencies. I've also included mail-order operations, like L.L. Bean and Ross-Simons, which make accessing your registry for long-distance friends and family as easy as dialing an 800 number. I'm confident *The Bridal Registry Book* will be your ultimate companion as you and your fiancé decide where you want to register.

Each store that appears in this book went through a thorough interview process. Listings were written based on information collected during these interviews along with anecdotes from recently married couples. No one paid to be in this book; therefore, none of the companies included influenced the write-ups that appear here. There might be some stores that you'd expect to find here but aren't in the book. That's because, for one reason or another, they wouldn't disclose the details of their registry program.

The Bridal Registry

The lore behind the creation of the bridal registry varies. Some say the concept was originally established when men and women were married at very young ages. Families and friends reasoned that since newlyweds lived with their parents right up until the day they were married, they probably didn't own enough furniture, dishes, and household appliances to outfit their new home. Others argue that bridal registries started as a marketing ploy used by jewelers who wanted a way to increase their bridal business from just engagement and wedding rings to fine china, crystal, and silver.

Whatever legend you believe, the fact remains that couples today are getting married later in life. According to the U.S. Census Bureau, in 1993, the median age for a first marriage for men and women was 26.5 and 24.5, respectively, up from 23.2 and 20.8 about 20 years ago. Even though they are older, there are still men and women who move directly from their parents' home into the one they're setting up with their new spouse. Likewise, there's an entirely separate category of the soon-to-be married—those who have lived on their own for years and enter a marriage with two of everything.

The Bridal Registry Book speaks to the needs of couples from both groups. If you need all the trappings to set up a home together, there are soup-to-nuts stores, such as department stores nationwide, that will meet your needs. And if you already have the basics and are looking for offbeat places to register, there are companies and catalogs for you as well.

The Bridal Registry Book is your comprehensive source of information on bridal registries coast to coast, perfect for your busy schedule. You may spend long hours at work advancing your career or in the library finishing up your degree. Because you don't have a lot of time to spare, you've become accustomed to various levels of convenience and expediency in everyday tasks. You rely on catalogs to buy your clothes, faxes to order lunch, and voice mail and E-mail to stay in contact with your friends. For you, the idea of spending hours trying to find the perfect bridal registry is not only unappealing, it's practically impossible. How can you possibly search out the best bridal registries that will be convenient to your guests across the country plus allow you to choose the gifts you'd really like to receive? Well, before *The Bridal Registry Book*, you couldn't. But, since no other book on the market speaks to your specific registry needs, *The Bridal Registry Book* is your perfect wedding planning companion.

How to Use the Store Listings

After you read through chapter 2, many of your general registry questions will be answered. Then you'll be ready to use the store listings to choose the store or stores where you'll register. In chapter 3 you'll find department stores, and in chapter 4 you'll find specialty stores. To make it easier to understand each establishment's services, there is an icon system, which will, for example, let you know where you can register via fax and which stores keep their registries on-line. Here are the icons that you'll see used throughout the book and what they mean:

register in person

register by mail

register by fax

register over the phone

computerized registry

sends catalogs to guests

provides registry cards

Using chapter 4 is as easy as combing the Yellow Pages for the nearest all-night pizza joint or the best health club. Like the Yellow Pages, stores are categorized according to their specialty or type. Specialty categories are listed alphabetically, and stores are listed alphabetically under each category heading. In the specialty store chapter, there is a cross-referencing system. Should a specialty store offer products that fall under more than one category, an icon will guide you to the section where the store's complete listing appears. For example, a large percentage of those registering at Lands' End are requesting linens, sheets, and towels. Therefore, Lands' End's listing will appear in the Bath and Bedding section. However, since Lands' End also lets you register for long underwear, you'll also find Lands' End listed in the Sporting Goods section with a "see also" icon that guides you to Lands' End's detailed listing in the Bath and Bedding section, like this:

LANDS' END   ☞ *Bath and Bedding*

You can also refer to the book's indices to find specific stores. One index organizes stores' names alphabetically, a second organizes stores' names by geographical locations (so you can see which stores are nearest you and your guests), and the third index organizes stores' names by merchandise categories.

2

Most Commonly Asked Registry Questions

Deciding where you're going to register—and what you're going to register for—is undoubtedly a big decision. Like most brides- and grooms-to-be, you're probably uncertain about certain aspects of registering, ranging from how soon before the wedding you should register to whether it is okay to register in more than one place. I've attempted to anticipate the kinds of things you'll want to know when selecting gifts and have provided answers to some of the most commonly asked registry questions.

Why should I register?

There are a number of reasons for registering, some that might seem selfish and others that are definitely altruistic. For starters, if both of you have never lived on your own before, you probably need items to set up your home. By registering for kitchenware, housewares, bath and bedding items, and even furniture, you and your future spouse are guaranteed to get your new home off to a great furnishing start.

But even if you have an established home, you should feel comfortable registering. A wedding is the perfect opportunity to select items that you might not otherwise be able to afford or have never allowed yourself to indulge in. For example, if you've got a kitchen fully stocked with casual dinnerware, take advantage of your guests' expectation that you'll register and go out and choose a formal china pattern, along with silver flatware and crystal stemware.

Ideally, your registering makes gift giving easier on your guests. Because today's wedding guests *do* expect couples to register, don't feel guilty about it. Instead, realize that by taking the time to select gifts that you really want and need, you're making it much simpler for your friends and family when it comes time to purchase a shower or wedding gift. It lets them feel confident that they're buying stuff that you'll be happy receiving, and they will appreciate knowing that.

Should I register at a department store or a specialty store?

The answer to this question really depends on your needs. Many younger brides and grooms choose to go the department store route because they prefer a store that can take care of all their furnishing needs. Because most department stores allow you to register from almost any area of the store—including housewares, bedding, furniture, and luggage—you can get literally everything you need to furnish your home. For people with eclectic needs, this kind of one-stop shopping can be a real convenience.

Specialty stores come in handy if you've already got most of your basic necessities and want to jazz up your home with unique items. Or, if you feel the selection available in department stores is too limited, specialty stores like Williams-Sonoma and Crate and Barrel can offer you cookware, dishes, and other housewares that are a little beyond the ordinary. Then there are specialty stores that really cater to the offbeat and specific interest—like camping stores, wine outlets, and lingerie boutiques. If these are the places that you'd really like to see your guests shop to get you wedding gifts, then by all means, register there.

Is it OK to register at more than one store?

Most of the brides I know *did* register in more than one store—usually a department store to take care of their basic home necessities (and because that's where their families expected them to register) and a specialty store or catalog for more unusual items. By registering at more than one store, you're giving your guests additional options in buying you gifts. Plus, since your friends and family may be scattered all over the country, it's great to choose one or two stores that can be accessed anywhere in the country, either via an 800 number or at store locations in almost every state (like JCPenney). This way, you're guaranteeing that your guests won't have a tough time getting a hold of your registry list and buying you what you'd really like.

I'm planning on registering at more than one store. Should I simply write duplicate lists for each store, or should I split the items up between the two stores?

There are a number of issues to consider before you even write up lists and submit them to the stores where you'll be registering. First, you should find out about each store's return policy. If, for example, the store will take back any merchandise whether it was purchased at the store or not as long as the store sells the same item, then you should have no qualms registering for all your items there. That way, you know in advance that if you get duplicates you won't have any trouble returning things.

You should also consider how many people on your guest list will actually be able to access the registry list at the stores where you've registered. If most of your family lives on the East Coast but you and your friends live in the Midwest and you've decided to register at department stores in both locations, then you should probably split the list between the two stores. For example: request 6 place settings of china at one store and 6 at another, instead of 12 at both. This way, should everyone decide to buy you china, you won't end up with 24 place settings altogether.

However, sometimes guests will buy gifts from another store. Maybe they found your wish-list items on sale somewhere else, or maybe they couldn't get to the stores where you registered. This practice can easily throw your registry plans out of whack, because you won't be able to keep track of what's been bought off your registry. Luckily, most stores will let you update your registry over the telephone—they understand that gift buyers often shop around. So, as soon as a gift arrives and you know it didn't come from the place where you registered, call the store and let them know. Most establishments will update your list in a timely manner.

My fiancé and I have lived on our own for a long time and have everything we need for our home. Is it still OK to register?

Of course it is. Just because you have your basic household needs doesn't mean you shouldn't register. Just look at the variety of stores, catalogs, and companies offering registries that I've included in this book. You might be surprised to learn that you can register for such wacky items as a barbecue pit (at Barbecue Hall of Flame, in Houston) and a boat (at BOAT/U.S. Marine Centers nationwide).

Since your guests and loved ones expect that you'll register (and since it will make their gift buying easier), take some time and think about what you and your spouse-to-be would really love to receive. Then, thumb through this book and look at all the offbeat stores that have registries; you might be pleasantly surprised at the options available.

For instance, if a romantic Caribbean honeymoon seems beyond your bank account, then register for a vacation at one of the handful of travel agencies that appear in the book. If you've been salivating over a new set of camping gear for your regular treks to the mountains, check out camping stores and catalogs, like Campmor and L.L. Bean, which both allow you to register for very outdoorsy items. Or, if you've been thinking about updating your CD collection, then registering at Tower Records might be perfect for you.

Should I register in the town where the wedding is, where I live, or the city where I'll be living after we get married? Or should I register in all these places?

The best answer to these questions is whatever will be the easiest for all your guests. Remember: even though they're buying gifts for *you*, you should make accessing your registry as painless as possible for them. One bride who lives in Chicago but grew up in San Francisco (where her wedding was held) registered at two places. She chose a well-known Bay Area store for her friends and family still living there, plus a nationwide house-wares store that guests in both Chicago and San Francisco could easily access.

Should I consider registering at a store that's not nationally accessible?

If you're marrying the boy next door and all your wedding guests live within a 50-mile radius of each other, then sure, why not? But the truth is like most families these days, yours is probably spread out across the country. Plus, if you and your groom-to-be went to colleges in faraway places, you've probably developed a network of friends living in many different places. Thankfully, most stores, no matter how small and no matter where they're located, are capable nowadays of dealing with out-of-town guests. They can describe your registry list over the phone, fax it or mail it to them, and then arrange to have a gift wrapped and shipped.

I really don't want to register, but everyone tells me I should for my guests' convenience. Should I just register for the heck of it and then return everything for cash?

I definitely don't advocate the practice of requesting gifts just so you can return them for cash. Not only is this in extremely poor taste, but what happens when you have a wedding guest to your home at a future date and he or she begins asking about his or her wedding gift? (Yes, I know this is tacky too, but guests are bound to do it.) One bride I know *did* return all her gifts for cash. Then, six months later, she had a friend coming to stay with her for a week who specifically requested that she'd like to eat dinner on the plates she'd bought the couple. Well, of course, those plates had long ago been returned to the store, so, in a panic, the bride went back to the store where she'd returned the plates and bought them all again (at a higher price, I might add). She learned her lesson.

In a situation like this, you should approach registering the same way as people who have lived on their own for a long time or who have been married before. Take some time and look at all the different companies in this book, and I'm sure you'll find a store that stocks stuff that you and your future spouse will really enjoy.

Or, you could choose to register in a store that offers a gift credit policy. That is, even though you register for specific items, when guests purchase those items from the store, no gift is sent. Instead, the store adds a cash equivalent credit to your account. Once all your gifts have been ostensibly purchased, you can use the total amount that has accumulated to buy whatever you like in the store. Be forewarned, however: stores that offer such policies aren't in the habit of writing you a check for the amount in your account. Instead, they'll issue you a store credit and expect that you'll use it.

How much homework should I do before registering?

Some couples like to spend weeks poring over

advertisements and articles in bridal magazines and compiling folders full of china patterns, serving dishes, and table linens so that they'll be well prepared when they finally go to register. Others just like to wing it once they get to the store. It really depends on your personality and your needs.

However, it doesn't hurt to do at least a little homework, especially if you choose to take the nontraditional route and register in an offbeat store. In this instance, you'll need to spend time thinking about the kinds of things you really want and will really use and researching which stores in the book will serve you best.

Even if you register for traditional things like china and silver, you should at least have an idea of what you don't like. One woman's fiancé told her from the get go that he refused to choose a china pattern that had baskets of fruit or colorful flowers on the center of the plate, things he found distracting when eating. When it came time to check out different dishes, they were able to tell the bridal consultant specifically the kinds of plates they didn't even want to look at and, within a matter of minutes, were shown a number of different patterns that had plain centers and simple borders. It didn't take them long to find a pattern they both liked.

Bridal consultants are there to educate you, help you make the selections that are right for you, and, ideally, speed up the registering process. If you don't mind a little hand holding, use them to their fullest potential.

Do I need to meet with a bridal consultant?

There are very few stores out there that require you to meet with a bridal consultant. So it's really up to you whether you want someone walking you through the store and helping you make gift selections. If you know very little about the quality of china, crystal, and silver, then you'll probably want to talk with someone who can educate you on products in the store, plus help you select patterns. Some stores have arranged it so that the bridal consultant can actually design a dining room table right in the store so you can see how pieces look when they're sitting on a table (as opposed to on a shelf).

How soon should I register?

As soon as your sweetheart pops the big question, your mind will probably begin racing with all the things you'll need to do before the wedding day. For many newly engaged couples, registering is right up there with setting a date, finding a location, and buying a gown. However, if you're going to have a very long engagement (over a year), you might want to hold off on registering until 6 to 12 months before your wedding. (Besides, even if you're having more than one shower, they probably won't occur until a few months before your wedding.)

Why should you wait? Because the items you choose for your registry list may be out of stock or, heaven forbid, discontinued by the time you're ready to walk down the aisle. One couple I know registered over a year in advance, around Christmastime, for a spring wedding that was two calendar years away. First off, many of the items on their registry list were gone from the store by the time the warm weather rolled around, primarily because the store had stocked seasonal holiday items. Then, to make things even worse, the following year their china manufacturer decided to stop producing their pattern. Thankfully, the bridal consultant at the store alerted them to this change and suggested they come back in and re-register. In hindsight, the couple realized that if they'd been less eager to register as early as they did, they could have spent just one day, instead of two, at the store picking out their china pattern and other assorted gifts.

If I decide, against all advice, to register a year in advance, how can I be sure that the items I've registered for will actually be available when my guests go to buy them?

Ask questions. When you choose a china pattern, a bath towel, or a brand of cookware, make sure you find out from the bridal consultant or store manager if the item is seasonal or about to be discontinued—they do know these things. If the answer is yes, then you'll probably want to choose something that isn't going to be gone by the time your guests get to the store. A best bet, at least in the china department, is to pick a pattern that the manufacturer has just debuted. Chances are it won't go out of stock or be discontinued any time in the next few years.

Nonetheless, you should always find out what kind of stock replenishment options are available to the store. Find out whether, if a situation arises in which your wish-list items are out of stock, the store can call its other locations to see if they have your items in stock and if shipping products from one store location to another isn't a big deal. If this scenario is impossible, determine how long a special order from the manufacturer will take. Some stores have secure relationships with their suppliers and can get merchandise in stock in under 2 weeks; other special orders may take as long as 12 weeks.

Are registry seminars that some stores offer really worthwhile?

If you feel you need a crash course in decorating and in using items for entertaining, yes, these seminars can help. But salespeople can also go for the hard sell here; so don't be swayed into registering right then and there, which is what they want you to do. You should shop around first and make sure the store or stores where you do decide to register will best meet the needs of you and your guests. (See Ten Questions to Ask About a Store Before Registering There.)

Perhaps the best part about going to seminars is that many include drawings for prizes donated by participating manufacturers. So you might just go home with a nifty gift. People walk away with things like an all-expenses-paid honeymoon, an espresso maker, or a sterling silver serving tray. Also, many stores give you a goodie bag just for attending. These bags often are filled with manufacturers' brochures and sometimes small gifts— I got a silver-plated frame from one seminar. This way, even if you don't win anything in the drawings, you'll have lots of fun stuff to go through once you get home.

Should I pick out items that I really like— and are really expensive? Or should I vary the price range of items on the registry list?

I can't say this enough; so I'll say it again: even though you'll end up benefitting from any gifts your guests buy you, you want to make their gift giving as painless as possible. Unless your last name is Rockefeller, you might want to avoid registering only for items that are completely out of most people's price range—including a $250-per-place-setting pattern of china, a silver pattern in which a fork costs $85, and a down comforter made exclusively in Sweden that costs $5,000.

Most of the store owners and bridal consultants that I interviewed for this book said the first question they ask guests who call or come into the store to access a registry list is "What is your price range?" Your guests are going to spend what they're comfortable with—not what *you* want them to spend. (One china shop owner in California told me that she purposely keeps her prices low so that when a guest comes in and wants to spend $100 on a wedding gift, a fairly nominal amount, she knows the bride and groom will get more bang from that $100 purchase than they would if her prices were outrageous.)

So by all means register for a few expensive things if you think someone might actually buy them for you, but be sure you vary your registry list so that your graduate student friends and your retired aunts and uncles alike will be able to find something they'd like to give you and can afford to buy. Besides, if you do register for only outrageously priced items, like a $250-per-place-setting china pattern, and you get only one or two place settings, you and your spouse will have to finish off the set yourself, and that could cost a pretty penny.

It used to be that you should register in time for an engagement party, but is that still true?

Definitely, especially if your family is accustomed to throwing such a bash. (In some social circles, the engagement party rivals the wedding itself.) Also, it's now common for couples to have not only an engagement party thrown in their honor but also two and three showers as well. So make sure you find out from your parents what sort of parties are planned down the road, and be sure to register at least a month in advance of the first get-together.

Do I need to register in time for my first shower?

Yes, yes, yes. Plus, since many of today's showers have a theme, such as lingerie, kitchen, or even patio, you'll want to be sure to register well in advance of these events so your guests have ample time to get to the places where you've registered and pick out a fun gift for you.

How long does it take to register? How much time should I set aside?

The time you'll actually spend in a store registering differs from store to store. At a small boutique, you can probably expect the whole process to take 45 minutes to one hour. At a department store or superstore that encompasses 50,000 square feet or so, plan on as long as three hours.

How can I convince my fiancé to go register with me?

Face it: some people just don't get into the idea of registering. Probably the best way to make sure your future spouse enjoys the registry experience as much as you do is to choose a store where you'll both have fun looking at the stuff. Since my husband's heart really beats fast at the first hint of sawdust, the best place for me to have taken him would have been a home improvement store. If your guy loves the outdoors, consider registering in a store that caters to an outdoorsy lifestyle. If your fiancé is really into sexy lingerie, suggest registering at a lingerie shop. Remember: you're registering for both of you, so make sure you find a place that offers items that you'll both enjoy.

What is the proper etiquette on getting the word out about where we've registered? Some of the stores have given me "We've registered at . . ." cards. Can my maid of honor insert these in shower invitations? Can I put them in wedding invitations?

Miss Manners and other etiquette doyennes find the idea of inserting these cards in any invitation so distasteful that if they could, they'd probably delicately remove their white gloves and smack you across the face if you did such a thing. But, thankfully, etiquette restrictions in various social circles have relaxed in recent years, and it's actually become quite commonplace to insert registry cards in shower invitations. Inserting them in wedding invitations is still considered a no-no, but, honestly, you should do whatever feels comfortable for you.

I recently received a shower invitation where the maid of honor had written at the bottom of the invitation itself, in lovely calligraphy, the names of the two stores where the guest of honor and her fiancé had registered. It was so unobtrusive that it was hardly offensive; in fact, I rather liked having the information given to me directly. This way, I didn't have to bother the maid of honor with questions about where the bride was registered. Instead, I had all that information at my disposal, and I could head right out and buy the bride-to-be her shower gift.

If, however, you are uncomfortable with having your maid of honor insert a card or include any other registry information in the invitation, rest assured that the word *does* get out about where you're registered. Mothers and mothers-in-law are notoriously good about spreading the registry gossip.

Should I have the store where I've registered mail catalogs to my guests?

Having the store do this unsolicited is probably a bit too pushy. But if the option is available, you might want to let your maid of honor know, since she'll probably be getting the word out about your registry and answering any questions your guests have about where you've registered. Or you can have her insert a note in the shower invitation, along with the registry information, that catalogs are available upon request.

How soon after receiving a gift do I need to send a thank-you note?

Even though I'm no arbiter of social etiquette, I was brought up with the notion that any time someone gave me a gift, I promptly wrote a thank-you. When I got married, I made sure that all my thank-you notes were written within two weeks of the big day. Etiquette allows for a month's leeway, unless a gift is sent before the wedding or given at a shower. Then, you should make sure the note is written and sent within two weeks of its receipt.

Remember: don't get the etiquette of thank-you-note writing mixed up with that of gift giving. That is, it's OK for guests to send a wedding gift within a year of your date of marriage, but it is not OK for you to take a year from your wedding to write thank-you notes. I know one couple who made this common error and ended up insulting almost everyone on their guest list.

Here's a great way to make sure that your thank-you-note writing doesn't slip through the cracks: bring the gift list and thank-you cards with you on your honeymoon. You'll probably have a number of hours to kill on the plane and in the airport. Why not use this time efficiently, to get your notes written? Get your spouse into the act by having him address envelopes while you write the notes and vice versa.

Also, check out this book's Appendix. There you'll find a registry checklist. On it you can keep track of the stores where you've registered, the items you've requested, any gifts received and from whom, and when the thank-you note was written. This way, you can be sure that your thank-you-note writing stays up-to-date.

What if someone says they sent a gift, but I never received it? How do I handle writing a thank-you note?

At the end of my wedding day, I was left with two gift cards that were not attached to any gifts—yet there were no gifts without cards. My husband and I hemmed and hawed about how we would handle this. We didn't want to accuse anyone of not giving us a gift, yet we didn't want to insult them by not writing a thank-you note. What we decided to do was call the two givers of the gift-less cards after the honeymoon. We said, "Gee, we're really embarrassed to call you about this, but it seems your card got separated from your gift at the wedding reception. We didn't want your generosity to go unthanked, but we fear that your gift was lost in the shuffle or stolen." It turns out one of the guests had forgotten the gift at home but had remembered to put the card in her pocketbook. She apologized profusely for her mistake and later sent the gift to us. The other guest had chipped in with another couple for our gift, and her card *had* become detached from the combined gift. She explained what had happened, and we promptly wrote a thank-you note. Because we didn't accuse either guest of any wrongdoing, we were able to rectify the situations—and write both thank-you notes—without any grief on anyone's part.

If yours is a situation where a gift was sent and it never arrived, you might want to call the gift giver, explain that the item never arrived, and have him or her call the store or company that sent the gift. There's probably a simple explanation for the gift's absence.

What do I write on a thank-you note for a gift I received but plan to return?

The proper way to write any thank-you note is to thank the person for the item and then briefly describe how you will use the gift. Write, for example, "Thanks for the lovely picture frame. We're going to have so many photos from our honeymoon that your gift will be a perfect place to display the fond memories of our trip." However, if you received something that you'll likely return, you could probably get away with either simply thanking the gift giver for the item by name but not explaining how you'll use it or writing a really generic thank-you note, saying something like "Thank you so much for your generous wedding gift; Dan and I were thrilled that you could join us on such a happy occasion."

Is there anything special I need to know about a store before I register there?

Just as you wouldn't walk into any bridal salon and buy a dress before you knew whether the store could provide you with the kind of dress-buying service you expected, neither should you register at any old store. It isn't easy deciding which store, catalog, or company can offer you the products you'd like to request. In addition, finding one that has a registry department that is well organized, understands the needs of brides- and grooms-to-be, and can guarantee a level of customer service that will make accessing your registry list and giving gifts easy on your guests can also be a challenge. Luckily, I've done most of the legwork for you. Still, I've compiled a list of 10 questions you should definitely ask a store's bridal consultant or manager before deciding to register there. Remember: these suggested questions are just a starting point; feel free to adjust the list so it best fits *your* specific needs.

Ten Questions to Ask About a Store Before Registering There

Do I need to make an appointment to register?
How soon after I register will my wish list be available for guests to access?
Will my registry automatically be sent to all your store locations?
Can I make updates to my registry list at any time?
How often is your registry updated?

What do you do to avoid our receiving duplicate gifts?

How will you work with out-of-town guests to help them access my registry? If necessary, can they make purchases over the phone and have items shipped?

How long after my wedding will you keep my wish list on file?

What is your return policy?

How big is your selection of china [crystal, bath and bedding, etc.]?

Department Stores

There are many different kinds of couples for whom registering at a department store is an awesome option. There are men and women who've never lived on their own before and are moving into a new home together. Obviously, they've got a lot of floor space to cover. There are also traditionalists who believe in the straight-and-narrow registering route and choose china, crystal, and silver from their local department store. And, there are couples who have established homes and are looking to update or redo their housewares.

The best thing about registering at a major department store is that you can request all of your basic household needs in one fell swoop. Plus, many stores let you request items in any of their departments, which can include everything from cosmetics to cookware.

In this chapter you'll find 23 department stores that roll out the red carpet for registering couples. I describe their service this way for a number of reasons. Since servicing the needs of the soon-to-be-wed has been their mission for years, many of these stores are light-years ahead of others in their registry service. For example, the bridal consultants of many of the stores in this chapter use handheld scanners to capture registry information, assuring accuracy, and then allow guests to access registry information via touch-screen kiosks. Most have locations in more than one state and/or a mail-order division—which makes gift buying easier on your guests across the country. Others stand out simply for the quality and range of products they offer.

Department Store Listings

BAYNHAM'S NEW ENGLAND MERCANTILE
180 Main Street   (603) 526-8070
New London, NH 03257

This upscale department store in the New Hampshire countryside, less than two hours outside of Boston and near many of the state's popular ski resorts, has taken covering the basics to a luxurious level. There are more than 15,000 items from 23 different countries in the store's 12 departments, which include High-Tech Hardware, Outdoor and Seasonal, Bed and Bath, Housewares and Gourmet Foods, Gifts and Collectibles, and Flower and Garden Shop. Products you can register for at Baynham's range from the very small—Caswell-Massey soaps and pewter picture frames—to the very large—a hand-carved Canadian wooden canoe and an AGA cast-iron cook stove from England (which you'll find in the kitchens of Princess Diana, Billy Joel, and Martha Stewart).

    Registering in person is a lot like attending a tea party. After taking a tour of the store, you'll be seated at a wrought iron table in the indoor teak gazebo and served tea and finger sandwiches while you complete your registry list. Even if New London isn't within driving distance, you can still register here. Just call Baynham's, and a salesperson will gladly take you on a verbal tour of the store. Because the store attracts so many seasonal customers who drop by on the way to nearby Dartmouth College or a ski resort, the store is used to dealing with out-of-town registrants and their guests. In fact, as soon as an order is processed, Baynham's mail-order division will immediately ship all gifts purchased over the phone.

The store is open seven days a week from 8:30 A.M. to 5:30 P.M. eastern time. During summer months, the department store stays open until 9:00 P.M.

BELK/LEGGETT

2801 West Tyvola Road   (704) 357-1000
(corporate headquarters)
Charlotte, NC 28217

Belk and Leggett, two family-owned department stores, which are partners under the Belk Store Services umbrella, have been taking care of the wedding needs of southern brides for more than 100 years. Both stores have fully stocked fine china and crystal departments that rival any department store in the Southeast, and it is the formal service pieces that most brides come here to register for. Brides can also register for bath, bedding, and kitchenware items.

Of the 257 stores, only 135 have bridal registry departments set up. You must make an appointment to register here; be sure to set aside two to three hours, as everything you register for is recorded manually. The store promises to have all your registry information available on its computerized system, which is automatically connected to all 135 stores, within 24 hours. Unlike other department stores, Belk and Leggett have not set up an 800 number for easy access to the registry. But a toll call to any of the stores with registry departments will allow out-of-town guests to access your registry, make a purchase over the phone, and have the gift sent directly to you.

Belk and Leggett have a fairly liberal return policy, but the stores do request that you make an appointment to bring in all your returns and exchanges. You can make this appointment at any store location.

The stores like to keep in touch with their registered couples. About six months after your wedding, you'll receive a letter inviting you to come back to the store to purchase any remaining pieces from your china, crystal, and flatware patterns at a 10 percent discount. The bridal consultants will also keep you up-to-date on any store sales.

Twice a year, Belk and Leggett execute weekend-long bridal events in partnership with *Elegant Bride* magazine, during which spokespeople from various tabletop companies give talks about their products. Perhaps the best part about attending one of these seminars is the free wedding planner you'll get.

Store hours vary by location.

Bloomingdale's

1000 Third Avenue   (800) 888-2WED
(flagship store)
New York, NY 10022

At Bloomingdale's, the entire department store is
at your registry disposal. You can go the
traditional route and request china, crystal, silver,
and items from the housewares department; or
you can ask for lingerie, furniture, luggage, and
cosmetics—it's really up to you.

When you register at one of Bloomingdale's
stores, you'll receive a bridal registry packet,
which includes detailed information about how the
registry program works, a form on which you can
write the names of people to whom you'd like
your registry sent (like your mother, mother-in-
law, maid of honor, and so forth), and a booklet in
which you can write your registry preferences.
The booklet covers the following categories:
formal china, casual china, formal stemware,
casual stemware, barware, formal flatware, casual
flatware, giftware, table linens, serveware, glassware, cookware, small electronics, cutlery, kitchen
basics, towels, bath shop, bed linens, decorative
home, luggage, and other.

What I like best about Bloomingdale's registry
is that it is prioritized. That is, you can let your
guests know that you'd prefer to receive, for
example, all your place settings of china before
any cookware items. Likewise, your guests can
prioritize how they want to shop for your gift.
They can request that your list be printed by
certain category only, if, for example, they're only
interested in buying you bedding items. Or, they
can have the list printed within a price range that

they feel comfortable spending. Both options are bound to make their gift shopping easier.

The store promises to have your registry information entered into its computers and available within 72 hours of your registry appointment. Then, guests can access your registry in two ways: by visiting a store or by calling the 800 number. Sixteen bridal consultants are stationed at this toll-free number, (800) 888-2WED. They can work with guests who want to make purchases over the phone, and you can call them to update your wish list at any time. Bloomingdale's will ship packages anywhere in the world. And if you happen to live in Manhattan, the store can arrange for a messenger service to make a same-day delivery.

Because all gift purchases are documented, returning items, if that's necessary, is a snap. If the product retails for less than $25, you'll get cash back. Otherwise, Bloomingdale's will issue you a store credit or let you exchange the gift for something else. Returns can be made at any store location.

Bloomingdale's likes to shower its registered couples with gifts. On the day you complete your registry, you'll receive a hardcover home planner book. In it are chapters on setting a formal-looking dining room table, what to look for in high-quality cookware, and the different kinds of duvet covers Bloomingdale's stocks. Each chapter includes photographs of sumptuously decorated rooms, and inside the back cover are folders in which you can tuck papers, fabric swatches, or anything else you might use in planning your home.

Besides giving all its registered couples the home planner, Bloomingdale's enters them in a variety of gift drawings. Each month, one couple wins an assortment of to-die-for home furnishings valued at over $1,000, such as a full tea and dessert plate set of Ralph Lauren china, a collection of Orrefors crystal, or a full line of cookware from fabulous French maker Le Creuset. In addition, each couple is eligible to win an all-expenses-paid honeymoon, one of which is given away every three months; in 1995, the destination of choice was the Four Seasons Nevis.

Bridal consultants are available at (800) 888-2WED Monday through Friday from 10:00 A.M. to 7:00 P.M. and Saturday and Sunday from 11:00 A.M. to 7:00 P.M. eastern time. Bloomingdale's store hours vary by location.

THE BROADWAY/EMPORIUM/WEINSTOCKS
3880 North Mission Road (213) 227-2514
(corporate headquarters)   (800) 626-4800
Los Angeles, CA 90031
🕴 🖥 📷

The china collection at these three West Coast department stores is quite impressive. Each stocks more than 200 patterns from a variety of makers, including Lenox, Mikasa, Wedgewood, Pfaltzgraff, and Dansk. China, crystal, and silver make up the store's biggest registry business, but couples can also register for items in housewares, domestics, intimate apparel, and cosmetics.

Many West Coast brides choose to register here because there are 82 store locations in five western states—Arizona, Nevada, California, Colorado, and New Mexico—all of which are connected by computer to the same registry. (California is the only state where all three stores are located; the other four states are home to The

Broadway only.) This is wonderful, especially if you have family and friends living scattered about the West Coast and the desert Southwest. Your registry is available at each location via a touch-screen kiosk located in the store's registry department.

Even though all three stores' registries are connected, information within the system is broken out by store location. So the only glitch guests might run into when accessing your registry is that they might need to know which store you registered at. For example: if you registered at The Broadway and a guest was accessing your registry from an Emporium store, he or she would have to specifically request a Broadway registry.

If your guests don't live near The Broadway, Emporium, or Weinstocks or even if they do and just don't have the time to get to a store to buy you a gift, they can call (800) 626-4800 to access the registry, purchase a gift over the phone, and have it shipped to them or directly to you. Every time a gift is purchased, your registry is updated, in order to avoid duplicate gifts. However, the stores promise to have the registry updated only within 24 hours of each purchase. If many of your guests wait until the last minute to go shopping and all converge on the store on the same day, your receiving duplicates is probably unavoidable.

Store hours vary by location. Personal shoppers are available at (800) 626-4800 to take gift orders Monday through Saturday from 8:00 A.M. to 10:00 P.M. and Sunday from 8:00 A.M. to 9:00 P.M. mountain time.

CARSON PIRIE SCOTT/BERGNER'S/BOSTON STORE

1 South State Street   (800) 374-3000
(flagship store)
Chicago, IL 60603

👫 🖥 ⬛

Even though there are 54 Carson Pirie Scott, Bergner's, and Boston Store locations across the Midwest, only 40 of them have complete tabletop and home store departments in them. Therefore, you can register only at one of those 40 stores.

The registry program here is really up-to-date. Each store is equipped with at least four handheld scanners that you can use to zap the sku numbers of the items you'd like to add to your wish list. Couples seem to prefer this self-guided registry routine because they don't feel as if a bridal consultant is always standing over them and telling them what they should register for. Once your registry information is downloaded from the scanner to the store's computer, it is available instantaneously at all 54 Carson Pirie Scott, Bergner's, and Boston Store locations.

You can choose from the following categories when registering: formal dinnerware, casual dinnerware, formal silverware, casual flatware, hollowware (serving pieces), glassware, cookware and bakeware, small kitchen electronics, cutlery, table linens, and bed and bath linens. In the china, crystal, and flatware department, these three stores have quite an extensive selection, with 220, 150, and 170 patterns, respectively.

If your guests don't live near one of the 54 stores in Illinois, Indiana, Minnesota, or Wisconsin, they can call (800) 347-3000 and reach Carson Pirie Scott's flagship store in downtown

Chicago to make purchases over the phone. Guests who purchase gifts in the tabletop, flatware, stemware, and dinnerware category won't be charged for shipping. Unfortunately, items from all other categories are subject to a nominal shipping fee. You can call this 800 number to get information on your registry, request that your list be mailed or faxed to a guest, and locate a nearby store.

When you register you'll receive a 44-page entertaining and home accessories booklet titled *Your Wedding & Beyond*, which includes basic information on how to choose items for your registry, a listing of Carson Pirie Scott, Bergner's, or Boston Store locations, a guide to anniversary gifts, and a chart on which to plot your family tree if you so choose.

Store hours vary by location. You can call (800) 347-3000 Monday through Friday from 9:00 A.M. to 9:00 P.M. central time.

DAYTON'S/HUDSON'S/MARSHALL FIELD'S
777 Nicollet Mall   (800) 243-6436
(corporate headquarters)
Minneapolis, MN 55402
♚ 💻

Legend has it that the Dayton Hudson Corporation, parent to Dayton's, Hudson's, and Marshall Field's, began its registry program in 1933, in the heart of the Depression, as a creative way for the betrothed to get practical gifts. More than 60 years later, the registry is truly ready to enter the 21st century.

When registering at many other stores, you must walk around looking at merchandise and keeping notes on the items you'd like to receive and then have them entered into the store's registry system, a process that can be very time-consuming. But this is not so at Dayton's, Hudson's, and Marshall Field's. Here, a bridal consultant accompanies you on your walk through the store. When you find products you like, the consultant takes out a handheld laser scanner and scans each item's sku number. It saves all the sku numbers in its memory. When you return to the bridal registry department, in one easy step, the consultant downloads this information directly to the computer. A few minutes later, he or she hands you your registry list.

Because the registry is fully automated, it is accessible immediately. Your list is updated instantly when someone buys you a gift so that you won't receive duplicate gifts. Also, buying you a gift is made even easier for your guests by touch-screen kiosks. These kiosks are located throughout the store and, with the touch of a finger, can print out a completely up-to-date registry list. If your guests don't have a lot of time to go hunting through the store but do have a credit card at their disposal, they can use the kiosk to purchase a gift and have it shipped to you all in one step. Or they can call the store's registry hotline—cleverly marketed as (800) 2-I-DO-I-DO—and order a gift. The stores send all purchases via ups, and delivery can take up to two weeks.

Because all three stores are owned by the Dayton Hudson Corporation, the registries at Dayton's, Hudson's, and Marshall Field's are all connected. With 63 stores in such diverse locations as Dallas, Texas, and Dearborn, Michigan, the stores cover a lot of shopping territory.

The Dayton Hudson Corporation stores strive

to treat their registered couples right and shower them with gifts from the day they come in to register. You'll get a wish book, which includes a beautifully photographed catalog of popular registry items. They range from formal china to area rugs to bedroom furniture. This wish book is housed in a gift registry booklet that opens with a four-page explanation of how the registry program works. It is followed by a simple wedding planner that you can use to organize your stationery needs, the purchase of your wedding attire, and the selection of wedding bands.

Two weeks after you've registered, the store sends you a thank-you gift of sorts: coupons and discount offers for 16 different areas of the store, including a complimentary makeover, 10 percent off men's pajamas, and 50 percent off any food item purchased in the Marketplace worth more than $20.

The store also will work hard to give you good service long after the wedding day. To make anniversary gift buying easier for your guests, it keeps all your registry information on the computer for a year after your wedding. Plus, if a bridal consultant finds out that your pattern is about to go on sale or be discontinued, as a courtesy to you, he or she will call and let you know.

Store hours vary by location. You and your guests can call the registry hotline at (800) 2-I-DO-I-DO Monday through Friday from 8:00 A.M. to 7:00 P.M., Saturday from 8:45 A.M. to 6:00 P.M., and Sunday from 8:45 A.M. to 5:00 P.M. central time.

ELDER-BEERMAN

P.O. Box 1448   (800) BEERMAN
3155 El-Bee Road
(corporate headquarters)
Dayton, OH 45401-1448

🚶 ✉ 📠 💻 ⬚

What's great about Elder-Beerman is the bridal
consultants at its 46 stores understand that today's
brides and grooms often register in more than one
store, even more than one department store. To
make the registry process easy for you if you
choose Elder-Beerman along with another retailer,
consultants welcome your faxing or mailing them
a copy of your registry list from another store,
which they will enter directly into their registry
system. This service is an excellent time-saver,
because this way you won't have to go through the
trouble of walking around a second store and
selecting items.

   If you do decide to make Elder-Beerman your
primary registration location, it is recommended
that you make an appointment with a bridal
consultant. He or she will provide you with a
registry form of all the store's departments and, if
you like, walk around with you and help you make
selections.

   No matter which registration method you
choose—in person, via fax, or through the mail—
your registry list will be up and accessible within
one to three business days. Your guests can access
your registry at any Elder-Beerman location or by
calling the store's special gift registry hotline,
(800) BEERMAN. Guests can make purchases
from all categories on your registry, except furniture and bedding, over the phone and have them
shipped to any location you choose. If for any

reason something purchased from your wish list is on back order, the store will send you a gift card notifying you of the gift order and its delivery status. The card always includes the name of the gift giver.

To avoid duplicates, your registry is updated each time a guest buys something. You're also encouraged to call the registry hotline if you receive anything on your registry from another store.

Store hours vary by location. You and your guests can call the registry hotline at (800) BEERMAN Monday through Saturday from 9:00 A.M. to 6:00 P.M. eastern time. An answering service will record any calls received after business hours, and Elder-Beerman will return the call the next business day.

JCPENNEY

6501 Legacy Drive   (800) JCPGIFT
(corporate headquarters)
Plano, TX 75024

🚶 ✉ ☎ 💻 ⬜

It's hard to believe that JCPenney waited until 1995 to throw its hat into the registry ring on a nationwide basis. In a short period of time, the store has been knocking the socks off engaged couples who decide to register with the company. First of all, JCPenney is one of America's only department stores offering a registry that has locations in all 50 states plus Puerto Rico. Of the 1,200 stores nationwide, only 700 offer a registry department on site; but you're not to worry: every single store is equipped with a courtesy phone that can connect you directly into the Columbus, Ohio-based registry center, where 75 operators are standing by seven days a week to handle registry inquiries. That doesn't always guarantee that they will pick up the phone in a timely manner, however.

Since JCPenney has set up a nationwide toll-free number, (800) JCPGIFT, you can register from anywhere in the country for any item in JCPenney's big book and its special wedding catalog. This catalog includes a limited selection of fine china, crystal, and silver from such manufacturers as Lenox, Mikasa, and Royal Doulton. Upon request, the company will send you a registry kit, copies of the catalogs, and a self-addressed, stamped envelope in which to return your registry list at the store's expense. Or you can visit a store with a registry department on site, where a registry consultant will take you around, scanner gun in hand, zap the sku numbers of items you'd like to receive, and then, in a matter of minutes, download this information to JCPenney's computerized registry system. Within seconds, your registry list is available nationwide.

Guests also have a number of options when accessing your wish list. They can visit a JCPenney store and get a printout of your registry from one of the touch-screen kiosks set up near the housewares department. This list includes item descriptions, current prices, the number of each item requested, and the number of each item already purchased. On top of the sheet is your own personal bar code, which a sales associate will scan in once your guest makes a purchase; it updates your registry on the spot.

Guests can also call the 800 number and have your registry list read to them over the phone, faxed to their home or office, or mailed to them. If necessary, the store will also send them copies of the catalogs in which your wish-list items appear. Once all this information is received, guests can call back and make a telephone purchase.

After your wedding, your registry information is available at store kiosks for only 90 days, but it is kept on file at the store's headquarters for two years. JCPenney wants to keep you happy after the big day has come and gone. To that end, the store has a bridal registry return program it calls Many Happy Returns. A few weeks after your wedding, you'll receive a letter from the store encouraging you to come back with any returns. The nice thing about this return program is you don't need to make an appointment with a bridal consultant, nor do you need to take your returns to the registry department. Instead, you can take them to any register in the store.

As an added bonus for registering at JCPenney, you'll receive a free 8-by-10-inch picture if you have engagement or wedding photos taken in their studios.

You and your guests can call (800) JCPGIFT seven days a week from 7:00 A.M. to 12:00 P.M. eastern time. Store hours vary by location.

MACY'S/BULLOCK'S
151 West 34th Street   (800) 459-2743
(flagship store)
New York, NY 10036

Complaints about the Macy's and Bullock's bridal registries used to be commonplace, mostly because even though the two stores were owned by the same company, their bridal registries were never really quite connected. For years, two different departments were running each store's registry program and rarely talking to one another. (Because of this lack of communication, one bride received 19 place settings of china!) All of that changed early in 1995 when Federated Department Stores purchased Macy's and California-based Bullock's and finally connected the bridal registries at the 110 stores nationwide.

There are still some glitches in the registry system. For example, getting your registry on-line and having purchases and updates show up can take as long as five business days. But, for the most part, the entire program is markedly improved.

Stores west of the Mississippi and about 20 Macy's stores on the East Coast now have touch-screen kiosks, which makes registry access easier for guests. (Guests still need to know which region of the country the bride and groom registered in.) There's also an 800 number that guests can call to find out what's on your registry, make a purchase using a credit card, and have a gift shipped. Plus, now that Macy's and Bullock's are owned by Federated, your wish list is also available on the registry system at Jordan Marsh stores in Maine, Rhode Island, New York, New Hampshire, Massachusetts, and Florida.

Macy's and Bullock's prefer that you make an appointment to register and that you set aside at least 90 minutes to get the whole thing done. A consultant will walk you through three of the store's departments—Tabletop, Housewares, and Domestics—and help you select items. When it comes to china, crystal, and flatware, the consultant will take samples off the shelves and place all the items, along with table linens, on a mock dining room table that the store has set up. This way, you can get a real-life sense of how well (or poorly) your china, crystal, and silver work with one another.

If you need to return anything after the wedding, you can do so for merchandise credit. Appointments for returns are preferred.

One incentive that Macy's and Bullock's stores offer that I like a lot is that they give a 10 percent discount on anything you purchase from your own list after your wedding. You have two months after your wedding to take advantage of this offer. The store also promises to match prices from like department stores, something your guests will appreciate. And if you end up having to finish off your china pattern yourself, you stand to save as well.

Store hours vary by location. You and your guests can call Macy's and Bullock's gift registry hotline at (800) 459-2743 Monday, Thursday, and Friday from 10:00 A.M. to 8:30 P.M.; Tuesday, Wednesday, and Saturday from 10:00 A.M. to 7:00 P.M.; and Sunday from 11:00 A.M. to 7:00 P.M. eastern time.

NEIMAN MARCUS

1618 Main Street   (214) 741-6911
(flagship store)
Dallas, TX 75201

There is definitely a sophisticated air to the registrants at Neiman Marcus. Bridal consultant Jack Lewis in the Fort Worth Neiman Marcus store believes that his brides are a little older than average, are perhaps registering for their second wedding, and want items that are of a higher quality than what other department stores offer. In fact, you won't find any Lenox or Mikasa china here. Instead, the store stocks such makers as Bernardaud, Christofle, Hermes, Limoges, and Steuben.

You can register at any of the 27 Neiman Marcus stores except the stores at Bal Harbour, Florida; Denver; and Minneapolis; which don't have tabletop departments or bridal consultants. However, guests visiting one of these three stores will be able to access your registry. Neiman Marcus requires that you make an appointment to register and upon your registering will present you with a handsome folder of information on products available in the store, an invitation for a complimentary makeover, and a number of brochures on creating the perfect paper trousseau.

Out-of-town guests who don't live near a Neiman Marcus store can purchase gifts over the phone, but the store does not offer an 800 number. Your guests will have to call the store where you registered or call the flagship store, whose number is listed above, for the phone number of the Neiman Marcus location nearest them.

Store hours vary by location.

SERVICE MERCHANDISE
P.O. Box 25130   (800) 251-1212
(corporate headquarters)
Nashville, TN 37202
🚶 ✉ 🖥 🎞

With store locations in 36 states and a mail-order operation, Service Merchandise is a great place to register, especially if you've got family scattered all over the country. You have the option of registering at any of the nearly 400 stores nationwide or over the phone via the 800 number. Many brides report that the personnel on the toll-free line are better equipped to handle registrations and have more time to spend with you than those in the store. No matter which avenue you choose for registering, be sure to have a catalog handy, because you'll need to record the sku number of each item on your registry.

You can request Service Merchandise's registry kit over the phone, which I recommend, since stores don't always have them in stock. The kit should arrive approximately two weeks after you've called to request it. It is packaged attractively in a simple white folder and contains a registry form that covers all of Service Merchandise's departments, including sterling flatware, sporting goods, and safety products, like fire extinguishers and smoke alarms. There's even a little something for the groom-to-be—an attention-getting information sheet letting guys know that Service Merchandise's registry includes such masculine goods as fishing rods and jigsaws.

The day Service Merchandise receives your registry form, it's entered into the company's computers. Because the registry is on-line, your wish list is available to guests at all stores and through the mail-order operation and is updated daily. What Service Merchandise doesn't tell you but you should be aware of is that its computer will categorize your registry based on the state where you register, if you register in person, not on the address that you list on the registry form (if they're two different locations). So, for example, if you live in Virginia and list your Virginia address on the form but are getting married in Mississippi and decide to register at a store there, guests will need to know that your registry can be found in the Mississippi section of the registry files, not the Virginia section.

Letting people know you're registered here is easy thanks to the preprinted cards the company gives you free of charge. Guests have the option of purchasing presents at a local store or through the mail-order division and of having the gifts shipped directly to you via UPS standard delivery. Sometimes Service Merchandise neglects to send gift cards along with the packages, however. So unless you know someone is sending you a gift, you may end up with a mystery package at your doorstep.

After your wedding, the store offers you a 10 percent discount on any items you registered for but did not receive, a nice added bonus to registering here.

Store hours vary by location. Operators are available at (800) 251-1212 24 hours a day.

STERN'S
Route 4   (201) 845-5500
(corporate headquarters)
Paramus, NJ 07652

Young people on the East Coast know Stern's as a sort of mid-level store where their moms shop for great bargains. But boy will they be surprised when they check out the store's registry program. Available only since September 1994, Stern's has gotten its registry service up to speed in no time, and it's a true rival to other department stores in the New York–New Jersey area.

What I like best about the Stern's registry is that it's still relatively unknown, meaning fewer crowds and better service. (But I guess it won't stay a secret for very long now, will it?) Stern's has invested big bucks in an impressive wedding book, which is given to all couples who inquire about registering. With its sepia-toned cover and velum pages, this book is first-rate. It includes guidelines on choosing and caring for china, selecting small appliances, and deciding on bath and bedroom accessories.

After you've had a chance to thumb through the book, you can enter your choices in the store's preprinted bridal registry booklet. Stern's promises to enter all your selections into its computers within 72 hours of receiving the information. Then your registry will be available at all 22 Stern's stores. Each night before the store closes all your guests' purchases are entered into the computer, reducing your chance of receiving duplicates. You are also encouraged to call with any registry updates should you receive gifts purchased from another store.

Store hours vary by location.

STRAWBRIDGE & CLOTHIER

801 Market Street   (215) 629-6000
(corporate headquarters)
Philadelphia, PA 19107

From its name, you'd think Strawbridge & Clothier was a department store that specializes only in apparel. But the store's name actually harks back to the two families who founded it in 1868. (The Strawbridge family is still involved.) In fact, because the store is still family-owned, doing business here seems to feel more intimate than at other department stores.

You don't need to make an appointment to register, but if you want to get the kind of personal, one-on-one service that Strawbridge &

Clothier has staked its reputation on for more than 125 years, I suggest that you do. During your appointment, a bridal consultant will meet with you and discuss your home decor. Then you'll be given a preprinted registry form, which you'll fill out as you walk around the store with the consultant. While the form covers only traditional registry items—china, silver, crystal, table linens, bath items, bedding, and cookware— you can include other items, like electrical appliances and intimate apparel, on your wish list. The entire registry process can take as long as three hours.

Strawbridge & Clothier keeps registry information on a centralized computer system; registry information is available at all 13 stores in Delaware, New Jersey, and Pennsylvania. Because all your registry information must be entered by hand, it takes about a week from when you have your registry appointment to when your wish list is accessible to guests. At about the same time your list is fully entered into the system, you'll be sent a copy for your approval.

Unlike the cryptic registry lists at some department stores, Strawbridge & Clothier's lists are broken out by category and extremely easy to read. Your list includes an easy-to-understand description of the products you've requested followed by "wants" and "has" columns that tell your guests how many of each item you've requested and how many you've already received.

Each couple who registers here gets 50 registry cards that they can insert in shower invitations and a copy of *Planning a Wedding to Remember* by Beverly Clark (Wilshire Publications, 1986), a spiral-bound, comprehensive wedding planner.

Store hours vary by location.

TARGET

33 South Sixth Street   (800) 888-WEDD
(corporate headquarters)
Minneapolis, MN 55440-1392

A recent informal survey revealed that Target is
quickly becoming a favorite department store
among engaged couples. Perhaps it's the cutesy
moniker Club Wedd, which describes the store's
registry program, that has made it one of the
first places people consider when it comes time
to register—more likely, it's Target's accessibility.
With 611 stores in 32 states, there's bound to be
a Target store located near any family and
friends who are invited to the wedding, making
this store one of the most convenient for all
involved.

Couples also like that registering at Target is a
very hands-on experience for them—and quite a
hands-off one for the sales staff. That is, no one
will be following you around when you register
here. Instead, all you need to do is stop by the
Club Wedd kiosk and follow the instructions on
the screen. You'll be asked to enter some basic
information about you and your future spouse,
including name, address, and wedding date, into
the Club Wedd computer system. (The worst
thing about the Club Wedd kiosks, in my opinion,
is a woman's syrupy voice that narrates all the
information that's printed on the screen. At my
local Target store, the volume of the narration was
way too loud, and I cringed every time I touched
the screen because I hated to hear that voice.)
Once you've finished this computer questionnaire,
stop by the guest services counter next door to
the kiosk. There you'll be given a pink handheld

scanner, which you can take with you as you traipse up and down the store's aisles.

The entire Target store is at your registry beck and call. Couples have been known to register for lingerie, lawn mowers, mountain bikes, VCRs, power tools, and patio furniture as well as the more mundane, like towels, teapots, sheets, and serving platters. When you find something you like, all you need to do is zap the UPC on the product and enter the quantity desired. The scanner automatically records the information.

Once you've covered the entire store, you'll bring the scanner back to the guest services counter, where all the information you zapped in will be downloaded to the system. This can take anywhere from 5 to 15 minutes. Then, you'll be presented with a printed copy of your registry. Go over it carefully to make sure item names and quantities are correct. Once any corrections are made and you've given your list final approval, then your registry will be available at all Club Wedd kiosks nationwide.

Besides the annoying voice, the only other downside to the Club Wedd kiosks is that when a guest gets a printout of your wish list, there are no prices on it, which makes it difficult for guests who have a specific spending limit in mind. Also, guests must remember to circle the items on your registry list that they do purchase and hand this sheet in when they check out; otherwise, your list won't be updated automatically—it will take about 24 hours.

On the upside, both you and your guests can use Target's toll-free number, (800) 888-WEDD, to obtain registry information. If you have any updates for your registry list, you can call them in to this hotline (or you can stop by a Target store, whichever is convenient). Guests can call the number for the Target store nearest them to find out if it has a Club Wedd kiosk in it (not all 611 locations have them at this time) and to ask any general registry questions they might have.

Target recognizes that your receiving duplicates and some unwanted gifts is unavoidable. To that end, the store has set up a liberal return policy for registering brides and grooms. About 30 days before your wedding, you'll receive a gift registry return card that you can use to return any Target items you received; you have four months past your wedding date to do so. With the registry return card in hand, you'll have the option of exchanging an item or receiving cash back.

Store hours vary by location. You and your guests can call (800) 888-WEDD seven days a week from 8:00 A.M. to 9:30 P.M. central time.

ZION COOPERATIVE MERCANTILE INSTITUTION

2200 South 900 West   (800) 453-GIFT
(corporate headquarters)
Salt Lake City, UT 84137

🚶 💻

ZCMI (Zion Cooperative Mercantile Institution) claims to offer one of the largest registry services in the state of Utah. With each store stocking nearly 600 china patterns from 23 different makers along with an extensive selection of flatware and crystal, that claim is not hard to believe. Couples who choose to register here do so because they have family and friends living in Utah and Idaho, the two states where the 11 ZCMI stores are located. If, however, you have guests from other

states who would like to make purchases from the
ZCMI registry, don't worry; they can call the store's
800 number and make purchases over the phone.

The store's registry program has been around
for more than 50 years. While registry information is kept on computer, a modern convenience,
the store's attitude about registering and weddings
is still a bit antiquated. For example, after a couple
registers and their wish list is entered into the
store's computer system, any updates to that list
must be done by the bride and only the bride.
Even if the groom was present during the registration and his name appears on the list, only his
fiancée has the authority to make changes to it,
either in person or over the phone.

In addition, in ZCMI's opinion, it is still a tacky
move to bring a gift to the wedding. So the store
has a hold program through which all gifts purchased for the registered couple are held at the
store until after the wedding. Instead of leaving
the store with a gift in hand, guests are given a
gift purchase card, which they can mail or
discreetly slip to the happy couple on their
wedding day.

While I do think the reasoning behind this
program is a bit outdated, it does benefit the bride
and groom in that they don't have to worry about
carting gifts from the reception to their new
home. This way, they can visit a ZCMI location
after they've returned from their honeymoon and
either pick up the gifts that their guests bought
for them or choose other items in the store. This
avoids their making troublesome returns as well.

Store hours vary by location. Registered
couples and their guests can call the gift registry
hotline, (800) 453-GIFT Monday through Saturday from 10:00 A.M. to 9:00 P.M. mountain time.

4

Specialty Stores

Specialty stores are a great registry option
because, not surprisingly, they specialize in certain
kinds of merchandise. Our cleverly captioned
subheads, like Home Improvement and Whole
Kitchen Kaboodle, let you know what those
specialties are; and, trust me, they run the gamut.
In this chapter, you'll find stores, catalogs, and
companies that offer everything from china to
camping equipment, woks to wines, and
honeymoons to hoes.

Bath and Bedding

There are a number of reasons registering at a
specialized bath and bedding store makes sense.
When you think about it, you spend one-third of
your life sleeping—and maybe quite a bit in the
bathroom. So why not have a well-appointed
bedroom and bathroom in your new home?

The bath and bedding stores listed here
usually stock a range of styles, colors, and designs
that you won't find in ordinary stores. The salespeople at these establishments eat, breathe, and

live linens and towels and can talk to you intelligently about the thread count of sheets and the plushness of towels. And in the case of companies like Bed, Bath & Beyond and Pacific Linen, veritable superstores, you'll find a huge selection of unique bath and bedding items.

In the case of a catalog company like Lands' End, you're guaranteed to get excellent service, because service is what makes or breaks a company like this. There's also another benefit to registering with a mail-order company: with catalog in hand, you can spend hours perusing the pages and deciding which styles and colors you would like to receive—all without leaving the comfort of your own home. Because operators are usually standing by late into the night, you can register when it's convenient for *you*!

ABC Carpet and Home
888 Broadway   (212) 473-3000
New York, NY 10003   (800) 888-7847
ᝰ

Don't let the name of this store fool you into thinking that all it sells is wall-to-wall carpeting. At ABC Carpet and Home you might just think you died and went to heaven. Why? Because when you step off the elevator onto the third floor of this loft building in Manhattan's Flat Iron District, you'll feel like you're stepping onto a cloud. Ahead of you, all you'll see is floor-to-ceiling shelves filled with fluffy down pillows, duvet covers, down comforters, bedspreads, cotton towels, and more by such makers as Wamsutta, Ralph Lauren, and Laura Ashley.

It is because ABC Carpet and Home has such an extensive linens department that the store decided to start its registry in 1993. Here, you can register for items from decorative home, table linens, sheets, basic beddings, and blankets departments and the bath shop. The store just added a tabletop department, which includes high-end fine china (Royal Doulton, Spode, Wedgewood), sterling silver, glassware, and table linens.

To help guide you through the process, ABC Carpet and Home provides a registry form. Once completed, it is kept on file and items on it are crossed off as your guests make purchases. The registry here isn't computerized, but there's only one store location and only two floors that have items included on the registry. Therefore, you probably won't get any duplicate gifts. Because of the intimate feel of the registry department, you can rest assured that your guests will get great service. Plus, your out-of-town guests can access your registry list and have gifts sent via the store's 800 number, which is available only during store hours.

ABC Carpet and Home is open Monday through Friday from 10:00 A.M. to 8:00 P.M., Saturday from 10:00 A.M. to 7:00 P.M., and Sunday from 11:00 A.M. to 6:30 P.M. eastern time.

ACE HARDWARE   ☞ *Home Improvement*

BED, BATH & BEYOND
715 Morris Turnpike   (201) 379-4203
(flagship store)
Springfield, NJ 07081
🚶 🖥 ⬜

When you walk into a Bed, Bath & Beyond store to register, you may not know where to begin—

these are *big* stores. With more than 70,000 items on display from a range of categories, Bed, Bath & Beyond refers to itself as "eleven stores, one address." Admittedly, that's a lot to take in. That's why it's recommended that you make an appointment with a bridal consultant, who can walk you through the store and help you make selections. For instance, he or she can recommend one brand of cookware over another and steer you toward items that you think are more in the price range of your guests. Even with this extra help, registering can take as long as three hours.

Within 24 hours, your registry list will be online and available at all Bed, Bath & Beyond locations in the United States; currently there are just under 75 in 16 states. Your wish list will also be available at three other stores Bed, Bath & Beyond owns: Bed & Bath Superstore in northern California, BB&Beyond in Worcester, Massachusetts, and Linens, Etc. in Cincinnati.

When guests come in to a Bed, Bath & Beyond store, a sales associate will always ask if they would like to have someone go around the store with them. If they're in a time crunch, this is probably an excellent option considering the stores' size. Guests can also request that your wish list be mailed or faxed to them and buy a gift using a credit card over the phone.

Because Bed, Bath & Beyond doesn't have a toll-free number or a separate mail-order division, your guests can call any store location when shopping for your gift. To make your guests' lives easier, Bed, Bath & Beyond's registry enclosure cards include the phone number of the store where you registered.

Returns are fairly simple. Just bring merchandise to any store location, and you'll get a store credit or cash refund.

Here are some of Bed, Bath & Beyond's departments and examples of items you can include on your wish list.

Sheets & Comforters stocks high-thread-count bedding ensembles by Laura Ashley, Adrienne Vittadini, Bill Blass, Wamsutta, Fieldcrest, and Martex, just to name a few. This department also includes pillows, duvet covers and matching window treatments. Shower & Bath Accessories has more towels than a hotel. The 100 percent cotton towels by Fieldcrest, Laura Ashley, and Martex, for example, come in 100 different colors and patterns. There are more than 300 shower curtains (including a series sporting Looney Tunes characters) plus matching rugs, toilet seats, hampers and more. Dinnerware & Glassware offers stainless steel flatware sets by Oneida and Reed & Barton and casual plates by Mikasa and Studio Nova. Over in Cookware & Electronics, you'll find pots and pans and other cooking accessories made by All-Clad, Cuisinart, and Farberware, to name a few. Lifestyle & Lighting is where the store keeps its furniture items, such as CD racks, coffee tables, and lamps.

Store hours vary by location.

CITY AND COUNTRY	☛ *The Whole Kitchen Kaboodle*
THE CONTAINER STORE	☛ *Home Improvement*
COOKWORKS	☛ *The Whole Kitchen Kaboodle*

CRABTREE & EVELYN
P.O. Box 167   (203) 928-1971
(corporate headquarters)
Woodstock, CT 06281
🏃

Most women register at Crabtree & Evelyn if they're having a shower with a bath or boudoir theme. And why not? Because the store offers a wonderful collection of high-quality English soaps, delightful creams, and lotions plus candles, sachets, and fragrances, gifts from Crabtree & Evelyn can make for a superbly scented home.

The registry here is not centralized through the company's home office in Connecticut. Instead, you visit the store nearest you and write down all the products you'd like to receive. The store manager will log that information in a registry book. If you know that friends will be shopping at one or a few of the nearly 200 Crabtree & Evelyn shops across the country, the store where you've registered will arrange to fax a copy of your list to those shops. They provide the store you registered at with any purchase information to avoid your receiving duplicate gifts.

Unfortunately, friends who don't live near a Crabtree & Evelyn store cannot access your registry or make purchases through the mail-order catalog. However, they can call the store where you originally registered and speak with a store manager, who will work with them over the phone. If your guests want to see the items you've registered for before making a purchase, they can call for a Crabtree & Evelyn catalog. They'll have to pay $3.50 for the honor because the company doesn't send them out for free (not a smart move in this age of mail-order shopping). Each Crabtree

& Evelyn store is set up to take purchases over the phone, so guests can buy items off your registry list using a credit card. The shop will gift wrap them for free and then ship the package via UPS to any location in the United States for a $5.00 bulk shipping fee.

Store hours vary by location.

CRATE & BARREL   ☛ *The Whole Kitchen Kaboodle*

DONECKERS   ☛ *Fine China and Crystal*

EDDIE BAUER HOME COLLECTION   ☛ *The Whole Kitchen Kaboodle*

FELISSIMO   ☛ *Home Decor*

GUMP'S   ☛ *Fine China and Crystal*

HOMEPLACE
31999 Aurora Road   (216) 498-0555
(corporate headquarters)
Solon, OH 44139
🚶 📷

When the creators of HomePlace opened the first store in Dallas in September 1994, they wanted to create a home decor superstore that also felt very much like a home. To achieve this effect, the store's exterior features a gabled roof reminiscent of a country home and each day coffee and bread are baked in the store's test kitchen (where cooking demonstrations are often held). These things make HomePlace actually look and *smell* like a home. You'll get the same sensation when you walk into any one of the seven other stores in Minneapolis; Las Vegas, Nevada; Scottsdale, Arizona; Oklahoma City; Hartford; Columbus, Ohio; and Buffalo.

It's true that the 50,000-square-foot Home-Place stores can be a bit overwhelming, which is why it's important to make an appointment when you want to register. "Our consultants walk every bride through the store," says Jacqueline Hominy, a store spokesperson. "We don't send them out alone unless they request it."

The consultants will take you to all the HomePlace departments. The departments include bathroom accessories, such as Egyptian towels and shower curtains; and bedding, where you'll find row after row of beds made up with the luxurious sheets, comforters, and pillows the store sells. Brand names include Crown Craft, Laura Ashley, and Springmaid. Most of the designs in the bath-room department coordinate with those in the bedding department. Other departments encom-pass glassware, where you'll find a 20-foot-tall wall of glasses by every maker imaginable; dinner-ware, including a Pfaltzgraff signature shop; cook-ware, where you can buy pasta makers, espresso and cappuccino makers, and bread machines (within this department, there are two signature shops, one for Calphalon and the other for Krups); ready-to-assemble furniture for all rooms of the house; and storage products.

HomePlace has a stocking system, which it refers to as a "category killer." "We offer every-thing in a certain line and stock enough so that there's never just one of anything in the store," explains Hominy. The store also offers open stock so that if you need to replace a plate from your

Pfaltzgraff dinnerware, for example, you don't have to buy a brand-new five-piece place setting. HomePlace has the one plate you need and will sell it to you individually. The same thing happens with the Oneida and Reed & Barton flatware it offers.

Getting through the entire store and completing the registry process can take as long as three hours. Thankfully, HomePlace consultants employ handheld scanners that instantly record your wish-list preferences. All this information is downloaded to the computer system once you've finished, and you'll get a copy of your registry list instantaneously. Another plus at HomePlace: there are touch-screen kiosks set up around the store, allowing your guests to get a copy of your registry list in one easy step. Nonetheless, Home-Place recommends that guests contact a consultant. This way, they can get pointed in the right direction and find the items on your wish list that they'd like to purchase—probably faster than if they had to navigate the store on their own.

As your guests buy you gifts, your registry is updated immediately at the cash register. The store also updates its registries every 24 hours, just in case anything slips through the cracks. When they buy something, your guests will be given a sales receipt without any prices on it that they can include in the gift box. This will make any returns easier, even though HomePlace's return policy is pretty easy to deal with as it is. You've got the option of returning merchandise for cash back, for credit to a bank card, for store credit, or in exchange for something else the store sells.

Out-of-town guests can buy things over the phone and have them shipped as well. The telephone number of the store where you've registered is listed on the registry cards HomePlace gives you to enclose in shower invitations. But since all the HomePlace stores are connected through the computerized registry system, your guests can work with any location. To find the store nearest them, guests can call HomePlace's corporate headquarters at (216) 498-0555. If there isn't a HomePlace store near you right now, there probably will be in the near future—the company estimates having 100 stores by the year 2000.

Store hours vary by location.

Lands' End

1 Lands' End Lane   (800) 345-3696
Dodgeville, WI 53595

You might think that the Lands' End catalog sells only rugby shirts and turtlenecks, but, in fact, the company, founded in 1963, originally sold sailboat hardware and equipment by mail. Since those nautical beginnings, Lands' End has diversified quite a bit, entering the bath and bedding business in 1990 when it launched the Coming Home catalog. Coming Home covers everything for the home, from sheets to shower curtains, window treatments to table linens. Almost immediately, loyal Lands' End customers who happened to be brides-to-be started asking if they could register for Coming Home's soft down comforters and fluffy cotton towels. Lands' End listened.

Today, the bridal registry service is run by a trained staff of specialty shoppers whose primary purpose is to walk you through the registry process. A specialty shopper will mail or fax you a registry form that covers only towels, sheets, comforters, blankets, quilts, pillows, rugs, and bathroom and bedroom accessories. If you'd like to register for items beyond those in the Coming Home catalog, such as monogrammed luggage or long underwear, you can create your own registry list and send it in. When your registry list arrives, someone from Lands' End will call you to let you know that you are now officially registered at Lands' End.

While the Lands' End registry isn't computerized, the department handling it is so small that you're pretty much guaranteed there won't be any duplication in gifts purchased. In fact, each time one of your guests makes a purchase from your registry list, a specialty shopper will actually update your list by hand. Your registry will be kept in an active file until three months after your wedding date.

Having Lands' End catalogs sent to friends and family is no problem. All you need to do is supply Lands' End with your guests' names and addresses. Lands' End has a 100 percent satisfaction guaranteed return policy, even on items that have been monogrammed. Friends who like to shop at the last minute will appreciate knowing that every order leaves Lands' End's Dodgeville, Wisconsin, headquarters within 24 hours after it is received (48 hours after if it is to be monogrammed), and can be packaged in a lovely silver and blue gift box ($5.00 charge) and sent via overnight and two-day delivery for an additional $20.75 and $9.75 respectively.

You and your guests can access specialty shoppers at (800) 356-4444 Monday through Friday from 7:30 A.M. to 11:00 P.M. and Saturday and Sunday from 8:00 A.M. to 11:00 P.M. central time, 364 days a year.

LAURA ASHLEY

6 St. James Avenue   (617) 457-6000
(corporate headquarters)   (800) 429-7678
Boston, MA 02116

🚶 💻

For the couple who dreams of having a home that
is decorated like a fine English cottage, Laura
Ashley is the perfect place to register. Through
the company's Laura Ashley Home division, you
can register for bed linens, towels, shower
curtains, lamps, fabric, window treatments, wall
coverings, furniture, rugs, luggage, table linens,
and tea and luncheon dishes. What's great about
Laura Ashley is everything coordinates, be it bed
covers, window treatments, or rugs.

You really need to register in person at one of
the stores that has a home section in it (not all of
them do). This way, a sales associate can work
with you to uncover the kinds of home items you
need and then help you coordinate colors and
fabrics. Because all 200 or so Laura Ashley shops
are connected by a state-of-the-art computer, your
wish list will be entered into the computer system
the very same day you register and will be available instantaneously at all stores. Even stores
without a Laura Ashley Home department will
have your registry information on their
computers, which means guests can visit any
Laura Ashley shop, even those that sell only
dresses, and be able to access your wish list.

Most stores should have a Laura Ashley Home
catalog on the premises so your guests can see
items before purchasing them. If the store doesn't
have a catalog and your guests are willing to
spend $5 (an outrageous amount, in my opinion)
to buy a catalog, they can call the company's mail-

order division (which, by the way, isn't connected
to the stores' computers and, therefore, can't be
used for making registry purchases) at (800) 429-
7678 and request one. At this 800 number they
can also reach a store locator service, which they
can use to find the store nearest them. Your guests
don't have to physically visit a store to buy something for you; all stores are able to handle and
ship purchases made over the phone.

As an added incentive to brides who register
with Laura Ashley, the company offers you a 10
percent discount on any gifts listed on your
registry that you do not receive. You have up to a
year after your wedding to take advantage of this
discount.

Store hours vary by location. Guests can call
(800) 429-7678 to locate the store nearest them 24
hours a day.

L.L. Bean   ☛ *Sporting Goods*

Lowe's Home   ☛ *Home*
Centers   *Improvement*

Pacific Linen
9170 Wadsworth Parkway (303) 456-8681
(flagship store)
Westminster, CO 80021
🚶 🖥️ 🎞️

Pacific Linen understands that many brides- and
grooms-to-be like to work on their registry list
without the help of a bridal consultant. And while
the 48 Pacific Linen stores have anywhere from
two to four bridal consultants on staff, the store
has designed a registry packet that lets you put
together your wish list on your own.

Inside, you'll find printed materials that explain how the Pacific Linen registry works, three forms on which you can write your preferences, and a five-part guide to selecting down comforters, pillows, bed ensembles, bath ensembles, and table linens, the most popular items on Pacific Linen registries. For example, this guide suggests how many sets of sheets you should ask for (three to begin with), how to select a color scheme (choose brights, darks, or pastels), and what kind of thread count you should look for in bedding fabrics (220 is the softest).

Once you head out onto the selling floor, you'll realize that you've got a lot to choose from. Many Pacific Linen stores encompass 30,000 square feet and stock thousands of items. Luckily, the registry form that you're working with is broken down by rooms of the house, as are areas of the store. These rooms include the master bedroom, master bath, guest bedroom and bath, dining room, living room, and kitchen.

You needn't register only for soft items, like linens and towels. Pacific Linen stores also carry bed frames and headboards, framed art, silver-plated flatware, casual dinnerware (U.S. stores only), and mirrors. When you hand in your registry list to a bridal consultant, as a thank-you for registering at Pacific Linen you'll receive a white wicker basket filled with Fieldcrest towels and scented hand soaps.

Your wish list will be entered in the store's computer system within a day of registering and is then available at all stores. Stores are located in Alaska, California, Colorado, Idaho, Kansas, Nevada, Oregon, Utah, and Washington plus the Canadian provinces Alberta, British Columbia, Manitoba, and Ontario.

Your guests will have an easy time accessing your registry, because Pacific Linen's computers can break out your wish list in the following ways: by room, by ascending or descending price, with everything that's been requested, and with just those items that have yet to be purchased. For example: if a guest wants to spend only $50, the list can be organized so that only those gifts that fall into that price range appear. Guests can request a copy of your wish list in person or over the phone. Once a purchase is made, your registry list will be updated within 24 hours.

Pacific Linen realizes that sometimes guests go elsewhere to buy gifts, so the store encourages you to call with any gift updates as soon as possible, in order to avoid receiving duplicates. However, if you do end up receiving more than one of something, you can return it and exchange it for something else in the store or receive the cash value of the item.

As a way to make you a long-term Pacific Linen customer, the store automatically enrolls you in its Purchase Points program. For every dollar your guests spend on your registry, you get one point. At a minimum of 100 points, you start earning gift certificates. At 100 points, you get a $5 gift certificate; 200 points, $10; 500 points, $25; and so forth. These gift certificates come in handy, especially if you don't get everything on your wish list and you want to finish it off. This way, you don't have to lay out any of your own cash. Pacific Linen also makes every engaged couple a member of the Pacific Linen Preferred Customer Program, through which advance notices of new products and special offers are received.

Store hours vary by location.

PRATESI LINENS

67 East Oak Street   (312) 943-8422
(flagship store)   (800) 332-6925
Chicago, IL 60611

👫 💻 🖼

Pratesi Linens is not the sort of place that you go
to register for everyday bedding. This high-end
store sells only its own line of Italian-made linens,
which are still designed by Pratesi family members
living in the Tuscan region of Italy. Most of the
bedding accessories are of an extremely high
thread count (over 200) and come with intricate
embroidery and tiny stitches. Besides sheets, the
stores offer marvelous cashmere blankets and
pillow shams, linen tablecloths and napkins, and
hand-embroidered towels and plush his-and-hers
terry cloth robes.

Pratesi owns and operates stores in New York
City; Bal Harbour, Florida; Beverly Hills,
California; Chicago; Boston; and Houston, Texas
(plus a variety of shops in such exotic locales as
Singapore; Milan, Italy; and São Paolo, Brazil);
each store keeps a separate record of the registry
requests local couples make. Like the linens it
sells, everything about the registry here is done by
hand. Your preferences are noted in a special
registry book, and your list is manually updated as
gifts are purchased.

If you've got friends and family living in cities
where there are other Pratesi stores, you can
request that your list be faxed there. By communi-
cating with one another on a regular basis, these
stores manage to keep any duplicate purchases
from being made. Guests who can't get to a
Pratesi store can have a copy of your list mailed,
messengered, or faxed to them. They can also

make purchases over the phone using a credit card and have merchandise gift wrapped and shipped. Pratesi has a 40-page catalog that guests can request for free.

Most Pratesi stores are open Monday through Saturday from 10:00 A.M. to 6:00 P.M.

REAL GOODS TRADING CORPORATION
☛ *Unconventional Items*

THE SEVENTH GENERATION CATALOG
49 Hercules Drive (800) 456-1177
Colchester, VT 05446-1672   FAX: (800) 456-1139

✉ 📠 ☎ 📖 ⬚

Couples who choose to register for their preferences with The Seventh Generation Catalog are usually those who are looking to set up an earth-friendly home and keep it that way.

What shows up on most people's registry lists is The Seventh Generation Catalog's unique collection of bath and bedding products. The GreenCotton line of sheets (200 thread count), duvet covers, cashmere blankets, pillow shams, shower curtains, rugs, and towels are all free of bleaches, synthetic dyes, and any wrinkle-resistant chemicals, which usually come in the form of formaldehyde. Many of these items come in a natural ecru, which Americans have come to recognize as the color of "green" fabrics. But some of The Seventh Generation Catalog's sheets are colorful, deriving their blues and yellows from ferrous oxide, a low-toxicity dye used in food. One of the shower curtains gets its color from onion skins. You can also request soaps, shampoos, and oral hygiene products that contain natural ingredients instead of synthetic substances.

Besides items for the bedroom and bathroom, Seventh Generation sells cool, down-to-earth stuff for almost every other room in your house. You'll find placemats made from raw jungle reeds, porcelain dinnerware that's guaranteed to be cadmium and lead free, energy-efficient lightbulbs, end tables for the living room, and a line of women's clothing made from the same GreenCotton as the bed linens.

Seventh Generation also offers its own line of cleaning products so you can keep your new home clean in a way that won't pollute or harm waterways. For example, the nonchlorine bleach is actually made from hydrogen peroxide—yes, the same stuff you used to use to lighten your hair. Well, it has the same effect on your clothing. But unlike chlorine bleach, which contains toxic substances, once hydrogen peroxide exits the wash cycle, it breaks down naturally into oxygen and water. The catalog also offers 100 percent recycled plastic trash bags, vegetable-based toilet cleaner, and toilet paper made from 100 percent post-consumer recycled paper. All of these items are available by the case.

When you decide you want to register with The Seventh Generation Catalog, just call (800) 456-1177 and request that a catalog be sent to you. Then, look through the pages, jot down what you'd like and call all the information in to the bridal consultant on staff (at extension 634). Or type a list up and fax or mail it to the catalog. On request, the bridal consultant will send you registry cards that you can insert in shower invitations.

Your guests have the same three options when accessing your list: they can get information over the phone, have the list faxed to them, or request that a copy of your wish list be mailed to them. They can have any merchandise they purchase gift wrapped (it's free) and shipped. Overnight and second-day delivery of any package is available to last-minute shoppers, but if The Seventh Generation Catalog sends it regular delivery, it picks up the tab for shipping and handling.

The Seventh Generation Catalog guarantees everything it sells 100 percent. If you want to return anything, you can do so in exchange for another catalog item or you can request a cash refund.

You and your guests can call The Seventh Generation Catalog's registry hotline at (800) 456-1177, extension 634, Monday through Friday from 9:00 A.M. to 5:30 P.M. eastern time. An answering machine will take messages at any other time.

YIELD HOUSE   ☛ *Home Decor*

ZONA   ☛ *The Whole Kitchen Kaboodle*

Fine China and Crystal

If you decide to follow the traditional route and register for china, crystal, and silver, you'll soon realize that you have literally hundreds of stores from which to choose. But who wants to register where everyone else has? That could mean getting through huge crowds and waiting in long lines. Instead, look through the store listings in this section to find a place that offers one-of-a-kind crystal pieces, like Hoya Crystal Gallery, or a place where you can find china designs that are unique and drop-dead gorgeous, like The Metropolitan Museum of Art. Or choose one of the smaller shops or mail-order catalogs that sell name-brand china and other items and offer great prices and service.

If you have wedding guests scattered around the country, selecting china from a chain china store or mail-order operation is an excellent alternative. Both can offer completion programs, a wide selection of patterns, and large inventories. And if your pattern is in stock, they can ship most purchases within 24 hours of receiving an order.

Because there are so many places offering china these days, I've checked out and listed some of the best shops and companies in North America.

ABC Carpet and Home ☞ *Bath and Bedding*

Al's Pottery, China & Silver
5700 Mayfield Road   (216) 473-1450
Lyndhurst, OH 44124   (800) FROM-ALS
🚶 ✉ 🖨 ☎ ▢   FAX: (216) 473-2040

Al's Pottery, China & Silver originally started as a simple shop offering local Cleveland brides a convenient place to register. But because the store has always had a policy that it will meet or beat prices from other stores and mail-order catalogs, soon the word got out that you could get great deals on china and crystal here even if you didn't live in Ohio.

To meet out-of-state customers' demands, Al's Pottery, China & Silver (which no longer stocks as much pottery as its name suggests) allows them to register at the shop either over the phone (by calling (800) FROM-ALS, which is available to customers outside the 216 area code), through the mail, or via the fax machine. In fact, the store will send you a preregistration packet that includes a list you can fill in with china, silver, and crystal preferences (you can also register for Calphalon and Cuisinart cookware here); registry cards to enclose in shower invitations; a brief history of Al's Pottery, China & Silver; and information on the store's policy on meeting and beating prices. Also you'll be informed of any special deals the store is currently offering.

The store has trademarked its own brand of bridal consulting—person-to-person registering. "We're not computerized because we always want you to deal with a human being," explains Ellen Lippman in the bridal registry department. So, if you visit Al's Pottery, China & Silver in person, you won't find any touch-screen kiosks or scan-ners. When you're registering in person and your guests visit the store, a sales associate is always on hand to help out. Likewise, if guests call from out-of-town, someone will work with them to get them your wish list (either by fax or mail), plus take an order over the phone, gift wrap the package for free, and ship the package to wherever they choose.

Even though Al's Pottery, China & Silver is quite proud of providing person-to-person service, if you happen to call the 800 number after store hours, you will end up talking to an answering machine. But, if you leave a message, a real, live human being should return your call the next business day.

Store hours vary by season, but the shop is open seven days a week.

ALMOST AND PERFECT ENGLISH CHINA
14519 Ventura Boulevard   (818) 905-6650
Sherman Oaks, CA 91403   (800) 854-5746
👫

When store owner Ruth Hertz opened for business in 1978, this store was a secondhand shop specializing in English bone china (thus the name). Since that time, however, Almost and Perfect English China has metamorphosed into a first-rate china shop that sells not only high-end English china, such as Portmeirion, Royal Doulton, and Spode, but china from manufacturers all over the world.

Perhaps Hertz should have moved to bigger quarters years ago. This tiny store's shelves are just teeming with china selections (don't bring a big bag with you; you might knock something over), and on Saturdays you can barely move through the cramped aisles. But she offers some of the best china prices in the Los Angeles area.

Not only can you register here for china but Baccarat and Lalique crystal as well. If you'd like, the store can also get you a special order of flatware, something it doesn't normally carry.

In some ways, the store still holds true to its roots and stocks some seconds. For example, recently it had in stock handmade pottery with which the only thing wrong was that the logo was stamped a bit off center on some of the plates. Almost and Perfect English China will also work with you to track down discontinued china items, in case you want to register for missing pieces from a family heirloom china set.

The sales staff here is extremely knowledgeable (most have been employed at the store for nearly 10 years) and will work with you in person or over the phone in setting up your wish list. They'll do the same with your guests, who can visit the store or call the 800 number, have a copy of your registry list faxed to them, make purchases using a credit card, and then have gifts shipped. If you need to return anything, you can do so for store credit or an even exchange.

You and your guests can call (800) 854-5746 Monday through Friday from 10:00 A.M. to 5:30 P.M. and Saturday from 10:00 A.M. to 5:00 P.M. pacific time.

BACCARAT

| 625 Madison Avenue | (212) 826-4100 |
| New York, NY 10022 | (800) 777-0100 |

👫

Baccarat crystal, around since the rule of King Louis XV, is best known for its simple yet elegant designs. While you can register for Baccarat in any department store and specialty shop in the country, nowhere else are your vast choices more apparent than at the gleaming Baccarat shop on Manhattan's Upper East Side. Here, you'll find an endless array of stemware, crystal sculpture, and Baccarat's line of jewelry, Crystal du Jour, all of which can be added to your wish list.

Because the shop is so small, the service is exceptional. Not only will a sales associate work with you in explaining the finer qualities of crystal, but if you'd like, you can take some reading material home with you. One brochure explains the detailed history of Compagnie des Cristalleries de Baccarat, still located in France, and gives you a crash course in what to look for in fine crystal. (This lesson will sound remarkably similar to the guidance you probably received when buying your diamond engagement ring. In fact, one of the terms Baccarat uses, like diamond makers, is *clarity*.)

Because there's only one Baccarat shop in America, the staff here is used to working with out-of-town guests who might want to access your registry list. The shop prefers not to ship crystal in order to avoid any unnecessary breakage, chips, or cracks in it. Instead, Baccarat offers a credit system. That is, the total dollar amount that your guests have spent to buy you specific crystal items is added up once your wedding date has come and gone, and you're given credit for that amount, which you can use to buy anything in the store.

You and your guests can call (800) 777-0100 only during store hours, which are Monday through Saturday from 10:00 A.M. to 6:00 P.M. eastern time.

Barrons

P.O. Box 994   (800) 762-7145
Novi, MI 48376-0994   FAX: (810) 344-4342

Barrons's mail-order catalog has been taking care of the registry needs of engaged couples across the country since 1975. The company understands that many Americans enjoy the convenience of catalog shopping and has made registering here as simple as possible.

All you need to do to get the ball rolling is call the customer service hotline at (800) 762-7145 and request a registration packet. About a week later, one will arrive along with a catalog. There are no bells and whistles on the Barrons registry form, which makes it all the easier to comprehend and complete. You just jot down the manufacturer and pattern of your formal and casual dinnerware, stemware, and flatware. Then, under the dinnerware and flatware heading, you check off the quantity of five-piece place settings you'd like as well as any other pieces you'd like to receive, like coffeepots, gravy boats, gravy ladles, and butter knives. Within stemware, you can choose from goblets, wineglasses, fluted champagne glasses, and iced beverage tumblers. There's also room on the form for any miscellaneous catalog items that you'd like to add to your wish list, such as Gorham crystal vases and Waterford bowls.

You shouldn't have any problem finding a pattern that you like, since Barrons claims to have more than 1,500 of them available. Once your form is complete, you can fax it back to Barrons or drop it in the mail. It can take as long as 48 hours after Barrons receives your list for it to get entered into the company's computers. Barrons can also supply you with bridal registry cards and your guests with copies of the Barrons catalog.

As long as your registered patterns are in stock, Barrons promises to ship any gift purchases within 48 hours. Otherwise, a gift card will be sent to you letting you know who has bought you what and that the item, now on back order, will be on its way to you as soon as possible. Barrons will keep your registry information on file for two years after your wedding, making it an excellent place for loved ones to shop for your anniversary gifts.

Barrons's return policy guarantees your 100 percent satisfaction. If you need to return anything, you'll get a full refund or a credit for the amount or you can exchange the item for something else in the catalog.

Customer service representatives are standing by at (800) 762-7145 Monday through Friday from 9:00 A.M. to 6:00 P.M. eastern time.

BED, BATH & BEYOND ☞ *Bath and Bedding*

BERING'S
6102 Westheimer   (713) 785-6400
(flagship store)   (800) BERINGS
Houston, TX 77057
🕴 ⬜

Couples love registering at Bering's because it's the kind of store where a guy can sneak off to the hardware department and create a wish list of power tools while his fiancée picks out china, crystal, and silver. In fact, word of mouth about Bering's extensive line of formal china and other items is what primarily attracts most brides- and grooms-to-be to one of the two Houston stores.

Both Bering's stores are warehouse-sized— about 10,000 square feet each—and include quite a variety of departments, all of which are at your registry disposal. There's the gift department, where you'll find china, crystal, and silver. In the gourmet department, you can get espresso machines, coffeemakers and, yes, even fresh roasted coffee. The housewares department stocks pots, pans, ironing boards, and vacuum cleaners. In the hardware department, there's every kind of wrench, drill, and saw to get a man's engine revving. The lawn and garden department has plants, planters, and weed wackers. In the furniture department, you'll find Chippendale chairs, dining room sideboards, and art reproductions.

Bering's is a family-owned store that's been in operation since 1940. Each location has a bridal consultant with whom you'll need to make an appointment to register. Both will walk you through the entire store and help you fill out one of the Bering's gift preference lists. If you register at one store, your wish list will be faxed to the other store so that guests have the option of shopping at either. Out-of-town friends and family can call (800) BERINGS to make purchases over the phone and have them shipped via UPS. Even guests living within Houston can shop over the phone. For these folks, the shop will wrap and deliver any gift for free. Bering's will even wrap and deliver a gift on the same day it was purchased, if your guest needs it that fast. In fact, one time a guest purchased a last-minute gift for a registered bride who was having an engagement party that evening. On her way home that night, a Bering's employee dropped the gift off, ensuring that it arrived in time for the party.

Bering's is open Monday through Saturday from 8:30 A.M. to 6:30 P.M. and Sunday from 11:00 A.M. to 6:00 P.M. central time.

BROMBERG AND COMPANY

123 North 20th Street   (205) 252-0221
(flagship store)
Birmingham, AL 34203

With six store locations in Birmingham, Montgomery, Tuscaloosa, and Huntsville, Bromberg's is pretty much the place Alabama brides go to register their china, crystal, and silver preferences. The downtown Birmingham store boasts more than 500 patterns.

If you've got your heart set on a pattern that Bromberg's doesn't normally carry, the store can work out an arrangement with you. "We'll go ahead and buy them the place settings they want, and we won't charge them anything until the wedding is over," explains Frank Bromberg III, a member of the sixth generation of Brombergs to be in the family business. "Afterward, if there's anything left over, the bride will have to agree to purchase the remaining stock." If it's a pattern you're dying to have, this is a pretty sweet deal.

You have the choice of registering over the phone (if you already know exactly what you'll want on your wish list) or in person. If you come in, one of the store's bridal consultants will be happy to take you around the store, let you set up various china, crystal, and silver settings on a table, and make up a packet of information for you to take home.

Each couple's wish list is entered into Bromberg's computer system and is available at all six stores. Guests can make gift purchases in person or over the phone, and delivery within the counties where there are stores is free. Bromberg says that many of today's brides request up front that actual gifts not be sent to them. Instead, they'd prefer to receive gift cards and have all their gifts held at the store until after the wedding. This system avoids unnecessary returns.

Store hours vary by location.

CHAR CREWS

8 Grant Square   (708) 920-0190
(location with best bridal registry)
Hinsdale, IL 60521   (800) 323-1972

Chicago-area couples who decide that a specialty china shop is where they'd prefer to register appreciate Char Crews, a family-owned store that specializes in fine china, crystal stemware, and flatware. There are five locations to choose from, one in downtown Chicago and the other four in the nearby suburbs Hinsdale, Barrington, Park Ridge, and Wilmette.

When you register at Char Crews (pronounced "shar cruise"), you'll have the option of actually arranging and rearranging your choice patterns, along with various table linens, on a dining room table. This helps you see exactly what your dishes, stemware, and silver will look like when they're in use, something you really can't get if you're looking at plates sitting on a wall or forks and knives sitting in a glass-topped display case.

Unfortunately, the five Char Crews stores are not connected by computer, so your wish list is mailed to each location and entered in the books there. This system causes a week or so lag time between when you register and when your list is available at all the locations. If you're in a time crunch, you can request that your list be faxed to the other stores to speed things up. When something is purchased, updates to your registry must be called or faxed to the other stores and this isn't always done immediately. So there's always the possibility that you'll receive duplicates. However, Char Crews accepts returned items at any location for a store credit.

You needn't make an appointment to register here; however, if you're planning to register at the end of January or July, call first—that's when Char Crews holds its semiannual five-day sale. During this sale, the store is extra busy, and you might not be able to get the attention you need, especially if you have registry questions.

If after you've registered here your china or crystal pattern is discontinued, Char Crews can put you in touch with companies that do nothing but track down pieces from discontinued patterns.

Store hours vary by location.

CHINA & CRYSTAL CENTER

5613 County Road 19   (612) 474-2144
Excelsior, MN 55331   (800) 432-4448

There are two reasons why you would want to register at China & Crystal Center: 1) you're a Minneapolis-area couple looking for some of the best local prices in china and crystal; or 2) an heirloom set of china is being passed down to you, and you want to receive additional pieces to the set.

This shop claims to have more than 15,000 pieces of discontinued and vintage china patterns in stock. What it doesn't have, though, it will find. The store has buyers across the country who are always on the lookout for out-of-production patterns at other china shops, antique stores, and estate sales. Anything a buyer finds must be in mint condition, or the China & Crystal Center wouldn't even consider passing it along to a bride or any other customer. Besides engaged couples, this shop's biggest business comes from families whose china patterns have been shattered during such natural disasters as earthquakes.

Of the active patterns that China & Crystal Center sells, there are more than 1,000 on the floor and thousands more in the warehouse by such manufacturers as Lenox, Mikasa, Noritake, Royal Doulton, Waterford, and Wedgewood. You can register here in person (an appointment is preferred) or over the phone. Guests have the same options for buying gifts and are encouraged to use the store's toll-free number, (800) 432-4448. The shop prefers to hold all gift purchases until the wedding is over so newlyweds can drive to the store and pick up all their merchandise at once or have it sent to their new home in one shipment. Anything that needs to be returned can be done so in exchange for a store credit.

Operators are standing by at (800) 432-4448 Monday through Friday from 8:00 A.M. to 5:00 P.M. and Saturday from 10:00 A.M. to 4:00 P.M. Store hours are Monday through Friday from 9:30 A.M. to 5:00 P.M. and Saturday from 10:00 A.M. to 4:00 P.M. central time.

CHINA OUTLET AND GOURMET GARAGE

443 Shore Road   (609) 927-5299
(flagship store)   (800) 538-6208
Somers Point, NJ 08244

👫

Register at one of the two China Outlet and Gourmet Garage locations in southern New Jersey and you're guaranteed to save 20 to 25 percent off retail. These shops stock more than 500 china patterns by all the major manufacturers except Lenox and Limoges. The Gourmet Garage part of the store offers Calphalon cookware and Henckels knives from Germany plus bread makers, toaster ovens, and various kitchen gadgets. All in all, the merchandise available in the combined 10,000 square feet or so at this shop will give you more than enough options when filling out your registry form.

That form is extremely simple to complete—just write in the manufacturer and pattern name of the items you like along with the quantity requested. Registering at China Outlet and Gourmet Garage can actually tickle your funny bone. That's because interspersed among the pages of the registry form are witty quotes about marriage. My favorite is this one from Groucho Marx: "The husband who wants a happy marriage should learn to keep his mouth shut and his checkbook open." Once completed, your registry list will be faxed to the other location, and as purchases are made, salespeople at each store will keep their counterparts up-to-date in order to avoid your receiving duplicates.

The stores won't fax your registry list to out-of-town guests, but a salesperson will work with any person over the phone by describing items on the list. Gifts can be gift wrapped for a $2.50 charge and shipped anywhere in the U.S.

China Outlet and Gourmet Garage's flagship store in Somers Point is located minutes from the Jersey shore, which causes the shop to become quite crowded during the summer months. If you must register then, do so in the evening, when day tripping beach crowds have already gone home. The other location, at 993 Route 73 South, is in Marlton, New Jersey, a Philadelphia suburb. It has a separate toll-free number, (800) 853-3472.

You and your guests can call the toll-free number at either location during store hours, which are Monday through Friday from 9:30 A.M. to 9:00 P.M. and Saturday and Sunday from 9:30 A.M. to 5:30 P.M. eastern time.

COLEMAN E. ADLER & SONS

722 Canal Street	(504) 523-5292
(flagship store)	(800) 925-7912
New Orleans, LA 70130	FAX: (504) 568-0610

Coleman E. Adler & Sons, in business since 1898, is another retailer that believes that the gift card system is the best way to handle purchases made from registries. Each time a guest buys something off your wish list, the store adds a credit to your account for the dollar amount your guest has spent. Therefore, no actual place setting is sent to you but a gift card is (so you can write a timely thank-you note). Then, once your guests have made all their wedding gift purchases, you're free to use the total dollar amount accumulated in your account to purchase whatever pieces you'd like in the store.

There are a number of benefits to the Coleman E. Adler & Sons system. When you register, you needn't know exactly how many place settings of china, crystal, and silver you ultimately want, because you won't have to actually select them until after your wedding. Plus, with no gifts being sent to you, you can avoid receiving duplicates and making returns altogether.

You don't have to utilize a Coleman E. Adler & Sons gift card system if you don't want to—it's just something they suggest to all couples. It's really up to you how you want the store to handle purchases made from your registry.

No matter which system you choose, your guests have two options for accessing your wish list. They can visit one of the three locations (there are two mall locations just outside New

Orleans) and make purchases in person. Or, they can call (800) 925-7912 to place a phone order.

The store's selection is quite impressive: china from 32 different manufacturers from around the world, crystal from 17 different makers, and silver and stainless from more than 20 companies. The store also promptly makes a special order for any items not in stock. Coleman E. Adler & Sons claims to offer a 30 percent discount off the recommended retail price of merchandise.

If you don't live in New Orleans and are considering registering here, the store will send you one of its annual gift catalogs. This way you can see some of the patterns it offers (as well as the prices) before you decide to register for your preferences there.

Store hours vary by location.

Compleat Selection

7592 South University   (303) 290-9222
Boulevard   (800) 366-9222
Littleton, CO 80122

Most of the brides who register at Compleat Selection are choosing what one store bridal consultant calls transitional dinnerware. "The dishes can go from breakfast to dinner and don't typically have a platinum or gold rim or any fancy edging to them," she says. "The colors they are choosing, however, are very vibrant." The store's registry leader is Villeroy and Boch followed by Mikasa, Noritake, and Lenox. She says brides are also looking more at functional serving pieces that are simultaneously decorative, like those made by Nambe and Wilton Armetale.

When you register at this suburban Denver

store, you won't lift a pencil. A consultant will walk you through the store and explain the various china, crystal, and silver pieces available. When you find something you like, he or she will take it down off the shelf and arrange it on the store's mock dining room table along with place-mats and candlesticks. Then you'll be asked to sit down at the table, pick up the pieces, and see how they feel to you. The consultant will also help you match various china, crystal, and silver pieces so that everything works well together. Once you decide on patterns, not only will your consultant add them to your registry list, but he or she will also take a Polaroid of the table so you can take it home and show it off.

Because the registry service here is one-on-one, registering can take as long as three hours. It's best to make an appointment beforehand and to understand that you will need to set aside a good chunk of time to get your registry completed. If you'd like to get a quick education on registering before you actually do it, check out Compleat Selection's semi-regular seminar Mysti-fied by Bridal Registry. The store also offers semi-nars on holiday entertaining, tea parties, and flower arranging.

Compleat Selection has a toll-free number, (800) 366-9222, that guests can use to purchase gifts from your registry. The store can describe items on your registry list over the phone or mail a copy of your wish list to anyone who requests it. Every gift purchased is wrapped for free and shipped via UPS anywhere in the United States.

One of the reasons that the sales staff here is so knowledgeable about china and such is that each employee owns at least three different kinds of china that the store sells. This kind of hands-on knowledge is something no manufacturer's brochure could ever give you. The staff at Compleat Selection try to get to know the brides that register there on more than just a business level and many times end up being invited to the registrants' weddings!

You and your guests can call (800) 366-9222 during store hours, Monday through Friday from 9:30 A.M. to 6:00 P.M., Saturday from 9:30 A.M. to 5:30 P.M., and Sunday from 12:00 noon to 5:00 P.M. mountain time.

COTTONWOOD CUPBOARD

2170 35th Avenue   (303) 330-4438
Greeley, CO 80634

This 6,600-square-foot store stocks every kind of china and dinnerware imaginable, and what the store doesn't have on its shelves, it will order for you. When you register for china here, the store will automatically make sure that it has at least four place settings of your pattern in stock to meet the needs of your guests. If, however, you register at the last minute, the store may have to give your guests gift certificates instead of actual place settings, because items are on back order.

After selecting china, as well as crystal and flatware, most brides head over to the store's housewares section, which is huge. Here you'll find items by KitchenAid, Krups, Farberware, and Cuisinart plus everyday dinnerware, glassware, and table linens. The store understands that its selection can be a bit overwhelming. Therefore, all registering brides and grooms are given the store's own booklet on how to set up a kitchen and dining room for the first time. It explains the

difference between bakeware makers, what kind of
gadgets come in handy (and which are just extra-
neous), plus tips on why you might choose ivory
over bone china.

A sales associate will accompany you as you
walk through the store, and once you find an item
you like, he or she will write on the registry form
the stock number and the quantity you'd like to
receive. That form is kept on file, and items on it
can be read to your guests over the phone.
Delivery of gifts is a free service, as is gift
wrapping.

When you register here, you'll be asked point
blank if you plan to register at another store; if
so, one of the bridal consultants will suggest that
you split your registry requests between the
Cottonwood Cupboard and the other store where
you're registering. This way, you won't get too
much of any one thing.

Cottonwood Cupboard is open Monday
through Friday from 9:30 A.M. to 6:30 P.M.,
Saturday from 10:00 A.M. to 5:30 P.M., and Sunday
12:00 noon to 5:00 P.M. mountain time.

DIAMOND CUTTERS INTERNATIONAL
4265 San Felipe   (800) 275-4047
Suite 960   FAX: (713) 622-3805
Houston, TX 77027

Diamond Cutters International is primarily a place
where Houston couples go to buy engagement
rings. Since the soon-to-be-wed makes up 75
percent of this company's business, it seemed to
make perfect sense that it should also serve the
other needs of engaged couples—mainly, bridal
registry, a service it began offering in 1991.

Because Diamond Cutters International is a small showroom located in a Houston bank building (as opposed to a retail store in a high-rent district), it doesn't keep a huge inventory on hand. This keeps the company's overhead to a bare minimum, allowing it to pass the savings on to brides and grooms who register here. Diamond Cutters International orders items on your registry list directly from the manufacturer and tries to guarantee that its prices will match or beat those from other stores.

Those living locally must make an appointment to register here. If you don't have the time to make it to the showroom or don't live in Houston, you can register through the mail, via fax, or over the phone. Because the company created its own registry software package, getting your wish list on-line takes only about 10 minutes.

Diamond Cutters International has relationships with every china, crystal, and silver manufacturer out there except for Waterford and Wedgewood. So if you have your heart set on registering for those two brands, this may not be the place for you. Otherwise, you should expect excellent service all around. (One bride whose fiancé bought her engagement ring here ended up registering here as well. Her experience was so positive that when word got out, 10 of her friends registered here when they got married.)

If you'd like, Diamond Cutters International can hold all your registry purchases for you until after your wedding. Then, if you live nearby, you can come in and pick them up; otherwise, the company will ship them to you. Returns are a bit tricky here, mainly because Diamond Cutters International doesn't keep a stockroom filled with china. If you happen to get more place settings from your registry than you originally requested, Diamond Cutters International will suggest that you try returning items to a department store (if you've registered at one as well as Diamond Cutters International). That's because Diamond Cutters International places a special order with the manufacturer when purchases from your registry are made, and, therefore, it can't send things back. If taking something back to another store isn't an option, on a case-by-case basis the store allows customers to exchange the extra items for something else it can order from the same manufacturer.

You can call Diamond Cutters International's toll free number, (800) 275-4047 during business hours, which are Monday through Friday from 9:00 A.M. to 6:00 P.M. and Saturday from 9:00 A.M. to 12:00 P.M. central time.

DONECKERS

409 North State Street   (717) 738-9500
Ephrata, PA 17522   (800) 377-2212

👫

Someone once described Doneckers as a specialty store that's grown to department-store size. Actually, Doneckers is more of a retail complex than a department store—each store front looks like one you'd find on an Old-World Main Street—which doesn't sound like a big deal, until you realize that Doneckers is located in the heart of Pennsylvania's Amish country.

It isn't the Amish who shop here, however. Instead, it's bargain hunters from Philadelphia and New York City who make the drive down to the tiny town of Ephrata, population 14,000. That's because the Doneckers complex includes shops that sell designer clothing, jewelry, and cosmetics plus home fashions, which is where most couples go to register for their preferences. There are also four country inns, a farmer's market, and a handful of restaurants on the property, all Doneckers-owned.

In the home fashions store, which feels a lot like a Colonial mansion, each room is dedicated to a different room of the house and is decorated with a different theme. You probably won't be in the store more than 10 seconds before one of the Doneckers personal shoppers greets you and asks if he or she can help you. This extra attention is anything but annoying—in fact, it's quite helpful, since the store is packed to the gills with great stuff and you could spend hours trying to find items that you'd like to add to your wish list.

You might want to begin with table settings. Doneckers doesn't offer run-of-the-mill formal dinnerware. Instead, it stocks many European china makers, such as Spode, Wedgewood, Herend (from Hungary) and Hutschenreuther (from Germany). Doneckers also offers reproductions of antique china patterns by Mottahedeh. Crystal comes from Baccarat, Lalique, Orrefors, and Waterford, and stainless steel and silver flatware is by Reed & Barton and French manufacturer Rentrenou.

Next, head over to the bath and bedding department, where you'll find sheets, towels, and bathroom accessories by Palais Royale, Liz at Home, Fieldcrest, Martex, and Royal Velvet. You'll also find handknit cotton throws. The store also has departments dedicated to living spaces and the garden, so you can register for redware pottery made by local artisans, crystal lamps, Lladro figurines and birdhouses.

If you'd like to see any of the items on sale at Doneckers shops in use, just walk over to one of the Doneckers country inns, where all the home fashions are displayed in the lobby and used to decorate the guest rooms.

Just as one of the personal shoppers here wouldn't want to see you wandering around lost looking for a china pattern, he or she won't let you lift a finger when filling out your registry form either. Instead, your personal shopper will write down all your preferences for you and then enter them in a specially designed notebook that the shop keeps just for registries. It should take about one day for your list to appear in the book.

Because most of the customers who normally shop at Doneckers don't live nearby, the store is adept at dealing with customers over the phone. They'll describe registry items to guests who call the toll-free number, (800) 377-2212, take credit card orders, and arrange to have gifts shipped.

Your guests can call (800) 377-2212 during store hours, which are Monday, Tuesday, Thursday, and Friday from 11:00 A.M. to 9:00 P.M. and Saturday 9:00 A.M. to 5:00 P.M. eastern time. Doneckers is closed on Wednesday.

FELISSIMO   ☛ *Home Decor*

GEARY'S
351 North Beverly Drive   (310) 273-4741
(flagship store)   (800) 4-ABRIDE
Beverly Hills, CA 90210   FAX: (310) 858-7555

🚶 ✉ 🏛 ☎ 📖

With 600 patterns of china, 300 patterns of crystal, and 280 patterns of silver, Geary's may well have the largest selection of formal dinnerware in all of southern California. Besides the selection here, what really makes Geary's stand out from other china shops is the quality of merchandise it offers. Manufacturers available include Tiffany & Company, Faberge, Ralph Lauren, Rosenthal, Hoya, and many more. The store strives to keep all its patterns in stock so that immediate delivery on gift purchases is always possible—Geary's would hate to keep any of its brides waiting for a shower or wedding gift.

You can also register at Geary's for informal dinnerware and various table accessories. Of note is the Deruta Italian dinnerware, which is hand-painted in festive colors. Matching handpainted place mats and napkins by American craftsmen make for a smashing table. There's also porcelain and handpainted dinnerware from Portugal, France, and England.

The Geary's North location, one block away from the flagship store, specializes in Lladro porcelain figures and Italian wood serving pieces, both of which can be added to your wish list.

You needn't make an appointment to register here, especially if you're going to do it from afar. Geary's registry form is simple to fill out and shouldn't take you more than an hour to complete once you know the names and quantities you'd like of your china, crystal, and silver.

Guests who often shop at the last minute will appreciate Geary's express delivery, a priority service that can get an in-stock gift to your doorstep within 24 to 48 hours of an order. Shopping at Geary's is made even easier for all your wedding guests thanks to the store's 800 number, (800) 4-ABRIDE. (This number is only available outside the 310 area code.) Any items you'd like to return, whether duplicates or things damaged in transit, must be returned to the store in their original packaging. You'll be given a store credit or allowed to make an exchange.

Geary's has been registering brides for nearly 70 years and likes to keep its past customers happy. To that end, your registry information will be kept in an active file for one year after your wedding and then in an inactive file for five years after that. This system makes it easier for friends and family who'd like to return to your wish list when buying you anniversary gifts.

Your guests can call (800) 4-ABRIDE Monday through Friday from 10:00 A.M. to 6:00 P.M. and Saturday from 10:00 A.M. to 5:30 P.M. Both Geary's locations are open Monday from 10:00 A.M. to 8:00 P.M., Tuesday through Friday from 10:00 A.M. to 6:00 P.M., and Saturday from 10:00 A.M. to 5:30 P.M. pacific time.

GEORGE WATTS & SON, INC.

761 North Jefferson Street   (414) 291-5120
Milwaukee, WI 53202   (800) 747-9288

Some in the bridal business say that it was George Watts who originated the concept of bridal registry back in 1917. As a jeweler who dealt often with couples buying engagement rings, Watts reasoned that a great way to increase his bridal business would be to allow couples to register at his store for gifts. Nearly 80 years later, George Watts & Son continues to offer engaged couples a great selection of china, crystal, and silver.

This 27,000-square-foot shop in downtown Milwaukee offers more than 1,000 patterns. Its bestsellers are Royal Doulton "Biltmore" china, Waterford "Araglin" crystal, and Towle "Queen

Elizabeth" sterling flatware. The only maker George Watts & Son doesn't carry is Fitz and Floyd.

Couples who register here are treated like royalty. Valets park their cars, sales associates guide them around the store and write down all their registry choices, and once their wish list is complete, the store treats them to lunch in the adjacent Watts Tea Shop. Even though this store is extremely highbrow, the prices aren't. George Watts & Son promises to meet or beat prices in a discount china catalog.

Guests receive excellent treatment as well. They can visit the store, where they too can take advantage of valet parking, or they can utilize the George Watts & Son toll-free number, (800) 747-9288 to use a credit card to buy a gift and have it shipped. Most items on any registry should be available for immediate shipping, since there's an on-site warehouse.

The staff here is extremely knowledgeable about formal dinnerware (one sales associate has been with the company more than 55 years) so you can be sure that you'll get the best registering advice possible.

George Watts & Son likes to keep its registered couples happy and offers you the following incentives. When you receive eight five-piece place settings of dinnerware, the store will give you a ninth for free; when you receive 16 stems of your crystal, you'll get two more for free; and when you receive eight or more four-piece place settings of silver flatware by Tiffany & Company, Buccellati, Christofle, Puiforcat, or Lunt, you'll get a silver chest for free.

Operators are available at (800) 747-9288 during business hours, Monday through Friday from 9:00 A.M. to 5:30 P.M. and Saturday from 9:00 A.M. to 5:00 P.M. central time.

GUMP'S

135 Post Street   (415) 984-9341
San Francisco, CA 94108   (800) 444-0450
👫

Gump's is not the sort of place where you should go to register dressed in a T-shirt and jeans. This store has been attracting the upper crust of San Francisco society for years, so to be taken seriously when you show up for your registration appointment, you should dress up for the occasion. It's definitely Gucci over The Gap at Gump's.

Saturday is the store's busiest day, so you'll need to call at least three weeks in advance for an appointment then. Otherwise, a week is plenty of time in which to secure an appointment with one of the store's three or four bridal consultants who are always on hand to assist customers. The registry department is on the second floor of this airy store, located steps off San Francisco's tony Union Square.

The entire registry process is extremely genteel. You and your fiancé will be seated in a plush seat at one of the mahogany tables and given a brief education on china, crystal, and silver. Then, you're free to walk around and choose from the hundreds of patterns that line the wall. You won't find lower-end china here; instead, Gump's carries a full selection of English bone china by the likes of Royal Worcester and Spode, along with silver and crystal by such fine makers as Christofle and Orrefors.

Your registry list needn't be limited to fine

dinnerware. You can also choose from bedding and bath accessories, terra-cotta planters, hand-thrown pots and platters painted in whimsical colors, and Asian antiques.

Gump's is happy to work with out-of-town guests by helping them access your registry list, describing items over the phone, taking credit card orders, and arranging to have items shipped from the store.

The store is open Monday through Saturday from 10:00 A.M. to 5:30 P.M. and Sunday from 12:00 P.M. to 5:00 P.M. pacific time.

THE HAY LOFT SHOPS

P.O. Box 260   (309) 579-3141
Old Galena Road & Route 29
Mossville, IL 61552

👫 ✉

If you're a big fan of Wilton Armetale metal dinnerware (made from an alloy of 10 different metals), then you've got to check out the selections at The Hay Loft Shops just outside Peoria. This gift shop, housed in a converted barn, offers one of the largest selections of Wilton Armetale items in the United States. The shop has more than 400 pieces in stock, ranging from beer steins to butter dishes to bowls, as well as dishes that have the sophisticated look of china but are made from Wilton Armetale's own special metal blend. Once a year, members of the Wilton family visit The Hay Loft Shops and sign original pieces for customers. Because of its huge Wilton Armetale selection that attracts shoppers from all over the country, personnel at The Hay Loft Shops are comfortable with registering couples via mail who don't live nearby.

You needn't limit your wish list to Wilton Armetale items. You can also add furniture pieces from the Williamsburg reproduction series, including lamps and book-ends, colored glass barware, American-made pottery, quilts, and formal china by such makers as Royal Worcester, Spode, Royal Copenhagen, and Royal Doulton.

A salesperson at The Hay Loft Shops will be happy to send a note to any of your guests to let them know that you've registered at the store. Those guests who prefer to shop by phone will get free shipping and gift wrapping.

If you register in person here, a month before your wedding, The Hay Loft Shops will set up a table devoted entirely to you and your fiancé. On it your wedding invitation will be displayed along with the place settings that you've registered for. The concept seems a bit tacky, but your guests, if they would like to see what your wish list items look like in use before buying them, may like it.

The Hay Loft Shops are open Monday through Saturday from 10:00 A.M. to 5:00 P.M. central time.

HESLOP'S

22790 Heslop Drive   (810) 348-7050
(corporate headquarters)   (800) 851-4545
Novi, MI 48375

When you register at one of the 13 Michigan Heslop's stores, you'll be seated in an overstuffed chair at a mahogany table where you and a bridal consultant will discuss your registry wants and desires. The consultant will present you with one of Heslop's bridal registry booklets, which you can read at your leisure, and then he or she will walk you around the store so you can look at the various china, crystal, and flatware displayed on the shelves. The selection here is enormous—more than 2,000 patterns on display. If you see something you like, the consultant can take a place setting down from the display and arrange it, along with placemats and napkins, on a dining room table that the store has set up in the middle of the selling floor.

The Heslop's registry system is computerized; the same day that you register here, your wish list will be entered into the computer system and available at all the stores. Since the store claims to have the largest in-stock warehouse of china, crystal, and silver in Michigan, your guests shouldn't have to wait for a special order when purchasing a gift for you. When a guest visits or calls the toll-free number, (800) 851-4545, to buy something, a consultant can just walk into the store's stockroom, pull the item off the shelf, gift wrap it for free, and either hand it over to the guest or have the gift sent on its way via UPS second-day air.

You might want to take advantage of the Heslop's Platinum Bridal Plan. When 11 place settings have been purchased, the store will give you the 12th for free. This plan also gives you additional discounts on registered items after the wedding. In addition, if you break a piece in your place setting, Heslop's can arrange to have just the broken piece replaced instead of making you buy a new complete place setting.

Your guests can call (800) 851-4545 Monday through Friday from 9:00 A.M. to 5:00 P.M. The store is open Monday through Saturday from 10:00 A.M. to 9:00 P.M. and Sunday from 12:00 noon to 6:00 P.M. eastern time.

HOYA CRYSTAL GALLERY
450 Park Avenue   (800) 654-0016
New York, NY 10022

Hoya Crystal Gallery, on Manhattan's swank East Side, stocks a to-die-for selection of, what else? Hoya crystal. Most couples visit this shimmering street-level gallery to register for stemware; many walk out with crystal sculpture pieces, serving trays, and decorative items added to their registry list.

Prices here are comparable to those at department stores, but the selection of items is much more extensive than what you would find elsewhere. That's why couples from all over the country who are big fans of Hoya Crystal register here.

You can create a wish list in person or over the phone with catalog in hand. (Unfortunately, only past Hoya Crystal Gallery customers receive the catalog for free. Otherwise, you'll have to lay out $5 for it.) Your guests can access your registry, make purchases, and have them shipped by calling the 800 number. If they like, they can have your gift inscribed with a personal message for an additional fee.

The store's return policy is a bit complicated. All items must be returned within three months *of purchase*, not within three months of your wedding date. So you might want to hold off registering here until just before your wedding to avoid any return snafus. Also, all items must be in their original packaging and in perfect condition (not too much to ask), and you have to have the name of the gift giver on hand when you return the gift. Otherwise, the store won't issue you a credit.

However, if you insist that it's impossible for you to find out the gift giver's name, the store will search its records for the information, although it may take a few days. Inscribed gifts cannot be returned.

The gallery is open and someone will answer the toll-free number, (800) 654-0016, Monday through Saturday from 10:00 A.M. to 6:00 P.M. eastern time. During summer months, however, the gallery is closed on Saturday.

KITCHEN ETC.

P.O. Box 1560   (800) 232-4070
(corporate headquarters)
North Hampton, NH 03862

The name of this New England–based chain of stores makes it sound like it's a kitchen-only store. However, most couples who register here do so primarily because of Kitchen Etc.'s great selection of china, crystal, and silver and its promise that prices on items in the store will be about 40 percent less than suggested retail.

You can visit one of the Kitchen Etc. locations in Connecticut, Massachusetts, New Hampshire, and Vermont to register. Or, even better, you can do the whole thing through the mail. Just call Kitchen Etc.'s toll-free number, (800) 232-4070, and request that a registry kit and catalog be sent to you.

Both registry kit and catalog are extremely comprehensive. The catalog has more than 100 pages of detailed information on china (both formal and casual), stemware, flatware, cutlery, and cookware. For example, the kit explains that Kitchen Etc. stocks 20 patterns of Wedgewood china and that it can make a special order for what it doesn't stock. It tells you straight out that such orders will take 8 to 12 weeks for delivery. Then, on the same page, there are drawings of all the pieces in a Wedgewood place setting plus the accessories, and a chart that tells you how much each piece costs.

The registry form is broken down into three sections, including a place to put the address where you'd like to have gifts shipped, a place to list dates of any upcoming showers or engagement parties, and 10 pages for listing your gift preferences from the following categories: bakeware, specialty gourmet, small appliances, cookbooks, gadgets, outdoor living (such as picnic baskets and crab pots), cookware, cutlery, kitchen accessories, bar and wine accessories, entertainment (chip-and-dip bowls and candles, for instance), formal dinnerware, formal stemware, casual dinnerware, everyday glassware, formal flatware, casual flatware, table linens, and kitchen textiles.

On the form you're asked to fill in the brand name and sku number of each item requested. Unfortunately, if you're registering from the catalog alone, the sku numbers aren't always apparent. Plus, the catalog doesn't include anything beyond dinnerware, stemware, glassware, cookware, and cutlery, so, if you can't get to a store and want to include items in other categories, you'll need to work with a bridal consultant over the phone to get brand names and sku numbers.

Once your wish list is returned to Kitchen Etc., either in person or through the mail, it will take seven working days before it's available on-line. But once it is, your guests can access your registry by visiting one of the eight stores.

Or they can call the 800 number and have it read to them over the phone.

For guests who prefer to shop via mail order, Kitchen Etc. will guarantee and insure the package when it is shipped. "If it never arrives, no questions will be asked. We'll just automatically reship the item," says Lois Matheson, manager of business development. Unfortunately for your guests, if they want to have the package gift wrapped, it costs an additional $7.50. The store also promises to update its registry every day before each location opens for business, helping to cut down on duplicate gifts being purchased.

There are some additional perks to the Kitchen Etc. registry program. When you register for eight place settings of china, casual dinner-ware, formal stemware, or formal crystal and seven place settings are purchased, the store kicks in the eighth for free. After all is said and done and you end up with duplicate gifts or too many place settings because people shopped elsewhere, Kitchen Etc. will take back any item you don't want, even if the store didn't originally sell it to your guest. "As long as we sell the same product, she'll get a merchandise credit," adds Matheson. Unsure whether something qualifies? Bring it into the store, have the sku number scanned, and if it pops up on the store's inventory, they'll take it back.

Kitchen Etc. also offers open stock. What this means is if, for example, you were to register and receive a certain china pattern and a teacup broke, the store would have just the teacup in stock, which you could purchase as a replacement. (If the piece isn't in stock, Kitchen Etc. would make a special order for you.) This saves you from buying a new complete five-piece place setting when all you need is one piece.

Your guests can call (800) 232-4070 Monday through Saturday from 9:00 A.M. to 5:00 P.M. Most Kitchen Etc. stores are open Monday through Saturday from 10:00 A.M. to 9:00 P.M. and Sunday from 12:00 to 6:00 P.M. eastern time.

KITCHEN KAPERS ☛ *The Whole Kitchen Kaboodle*

LANAC SALES
73 Canal Street
New York, NY 10002

(212) 725-6422
(800) 522-0047
FAX: (212) 925-8175

Right in the Lanac Sales catalog, the company boasts about its reputation for "high quality, low prices, and expert services." I'd have to agree on all three points, since this discounter sells high-end china, crystal, and flatware, such as Spode, Bernardaud and Gorham. Plus, it says right in print that it "will match or beat any advertised price." And if you compare Lanac Sales's prices with those found at most retail and department stores, you'll see that Lanac does indeed offer a good deal.

Should you decide to register here, you can do so at the store's cramped quarters in Manhattan or via the catalog. (Lanac Sales also stocks Calphalon cookware and Cuisinart electrical appliances, which you can register for as well.) Since the registry is computerized, your list is available right away, and your guests can access it by calling (800) 522-0047. Each time someone buys an item off your registry, Lanac Sales will send you a letter letting you know who bought you what and notifying you of all the remaining items on your registry. This way, you can keep track of gift purchases and promptly write thank-you notes.

Lanac Sales has three different registry incentive programs. Through the Silver Registry plan, when $600 worth of items are purchased from your registry, you'll receive an etched glass decanter and six matching wine goblets plus a video on napkin folding as a gift. Through the Gold Registry plan, when $1,200 worth of merchandise is purchased from your registry, you'll get a silver-plated ice bucket with matching tongs, plus the video on napkin folding. Through the Platinum Registry plan, when $2,300 is spent on your registry, Lanac will give you a four-piece silver-plated tea/coffee hostess set that includes a coffee/tea pot, sugar bowl, creamer, and tray, along with the video on napkin folding.

I have just two reservations about Lanac Sales. First, it took the store more than a month to mail me a catalog. Granted, I called just before Passover, and since this company is run by religious Jewish men and women who close down for every Jewish holiday, I can imagine that this was the reason for the delay. And, second, the store doesn't take any returns on bridal registry items, so you've really got to love the stuff you register for here.

Your guests can call (800) 522-0047 during store hours, which are Monday through Thursday from 9:00 A.M. to 6:00 P.M.; Friday from 9:00 A.M. to 2:00 P.M., and Sunday from 10:00 A.M. to 5:00 P.M. eastern time.

LENOX
100 Lenox Drive   (800) 423-8946
(corporate headquarters)
Lawrenceville, NJ 08648
🚶

If you've got your heart set on registering for
Lenox china and you live near one of the 21 outlet
stores across the country, then you really ought to
consider registering at one of these locations. It's
something you must do in person, however, since
each of the stores is independently run.

But be forewarned: Registries are handled in
an arcane way at the outlets. For example, they
won't mail or fax a copy of your registry list to
your guests. Plus, the registry list doesn't include
any of the deeply discounted prices. So when a
guest calls and asks about prices, a salesperson
will probably put him or her on hold, run out to
the sales floor, check on the price, and then report
back to that person. If your guest needs to check
on a bunch of items, the process could easily
become tedious.

But in exchange for a little patience and
understanding, you'll find a huge selection of
casual and formal dinnerware along with Gorham
stainless steel flatware and crystal. And your
guests will be pleasantly surprised by the great
prices they'll find. A friend of mine registered at
the Lenox store at the Birch Run outlet mall in
Michigan, and a five-piece place setting of her
china was more than $10 cheaper at the outlet
than at the local department store where she'd also
registered.

Besides Michigan, there are Lenox outlet
stores in Arizona, California, Colorado, Florida,

Georgia, Maine, Missouri, New Hampshire, New York, Ohio, Pennsylvania, Tennessee, Texas, Virginia, and Wisconsin.

Each Lenox store is capable of shipping items purchased over the phone via UPS insured delivery, and many will charge your guests an affordable, flat shipping fee. At the Birch Run store, for example, that fee was $6.00 per every $100 spent on merchandise.

To find the outlet store nearest you, you can call the company's toll-free store locator number. Since Lenox is one of the most popular brands for couples to register for these days, this line tends to get extremely busy, so don't be surprised if you're on hold for 10 minutes before an operator picks up.

You can call the store locator number, (800) 423-8946, Monday through Friday from 9:00 A.M. to 5:00 P.M. eastern time. Store hours vary by outlet location.

METROPOLITAN MUSEUM OF ART SHOPS ☛ *Home Decor*

MICHAEL C. FINA

580 Fifth Avenue   (212) 869-5050
New York, NY 10036   (800) 288-FINA

🚶 ☎ 💻 📖 🎞

Michael C. Fina is known in New York City and around the country as having one of the more extensive selections of china, crystal, and flatware—the store has access to more than 5,000 patterns. Unfortunately, what this shop located in the Diamond District is *not* known for is its extensive stock. That means that most of the items you register for must be special ordered, and delivery can take as long as eight weeks. So if you're going to register just a few weeks before your wedding, then you might want to rule out Michael C. Fina. But if you're like most couples who register three to six months before they're getting married, then definitely check this place out.

Because of its reputation for great prices, Michael C. Fina works with out-of-state customers all the time. To register here, call (800) 288-FINA, and you can describe your wish-list choices over the phone. Or if you'd like to see some of the merchandise beforehand, you can request that a catalog be sent to you. The catalog comes complete with a bridal registry planner and price list.

During high registry season, namely the spring months, your call to the registry line might be met by the store's answering service. Just leave your name and number, and someone will call you back within a business day. Once you're ready to register, an operator will capture a description of all the items you want to add to your wish list and immediately enter this information into the store's computerized registry system. As a gift to you, the store gives all registered brides a silver-plated picture frame.

Your registry requests needn't be limited to china, crystal, and silver: Michael C. Fina also offers competitive prices on pasta makers, bread machines, Calphalon cookware, and cappuccino makers.

Guests can request a catalog be sent to them along with a copy of your registry list. Because Michael C. Fina promises to match competitors' prices, it doesn't include any prices on the registry list. The shop has a separate line for taking orders, (800) BUY-FINA. If your guests order something that Michael C. Fina doesn't have in stock, which is quite likely, they'll be asked to pay 50 percent of the order price up front and then the remaining 50 percent when the item arrives at the shop. (In the meantime, the store will send you a gift card letting you know that something has been purchased from your registry.) Once the order comes in, it can be shipped out (the store charges a $6 flat shipping charge for each $200 of an order) or picked up.

Michael C. Fina keeps your registry on file for up to three years after you've registered, allowing the store to notify you when it or the manufacturer of your china, crystal, or flatware is running a sale.

You and your guests can call (800) 288-FINA and (800) BUY-FINA during store hours, which are Monday through Wednesday from 9:30 A.M. to 6:00 P.M., Thursday from 9:30 A.M. to 7:00 P.M., Friday from 9:30 A.M. to 6:00 P.M., and Saturday from 10:30 A.M. to 6:00 P.M. eastern time.

MIDAS CHINA & SILVER

4315 Walney Road   (703) 802-3233
(corporate headquarters)   (800) 368-3153
Chantilly, VA 22021

Midas China & Silver tries to separate itself from other mail-order catalogers in a number of ways. First, it claims to sell its merchandise at a savings up to 70 percent off manufacturers' suggested retail prices. Second, if you register at one of its two Washington, D.C.–area stores or via its mail-order operation, the company will mail your invitations for you at its expense. The catch is that you have to agree to let the company enclose its "The bride and groom have registered at Midas China & Silver" cards. And, third, you have up to a year after your wedding to return registry items. (Most places give six months.)

Midas China & Silver carries all the popular makers of china, crystal, and flatware—Baccarat, Lenox, Noritake, and so forth—and offers an extensive line of Waterford crystal giftware, such as bowls, vases, and serving accessories. As guests buy gifts, the company's computer system will automatically generate an updated version of your registry list, which is mailed to you.

The company admits that it cannot possibly stock every item at all times, and therefore, back orders do happen. Sometimes your guests, who can purchase gifts in person at one of the two stores or by calling (800) 368-3153, may have to wait 4 to 12 weeks for delivery of a gift. They will not be charged until the item actually arrives, however. When something is on back order, Midas will send you a card letting you know that a gift is out of stock and should be arriving shortly.

In its catalog, Midas tells you beforehand that there are certain manufacturers that in its experience have been slow with back orders. They are Noritake, Royal Worcester, Spode, Mikasa, Wedgewood, Lenox, Aynsley, and Estate Silver.

Your guests can call (800) 368-3153 during store hours, which are Monday through Friday from 9:00 A.M. to 6:00 P.M. and Saturday from 10:00 A.M. to 4:00 P.M. eastern time.

NAT SCHWARTZ & CO.

549 Broadway   (800) 526-1440
Bayonne, NJ 07002

When you register at Nat Schwartz & Co., it's entirely possible that you'll end up dealing with a member of the Schwartz family. Because this is a tight-knit, family-run business, the type of service you can expect to get here is more mom-and-pop than big business. One bride called the company's 800 number to request information on registering, and, unfortunately, had to leave a message on the answering machine, because everyone was busy. But an hour later, Alan Schwartz, son of the owner, called her back and spent 30 minutes talking with her about her registry needs. "It's not unheard of for us to spend two hours on the phone counseling someone on her registry decisions," Alan told me.

You get the same kind of one-on-one attention when you register in person, and an appointment is definitely recommended. Many out-of-town brides who come to New York on business schedule an appointment at Nat Schwartz & Co. either right after they land at Newark Airport or right before they fly out. That's because the airport is a quick five-minute drive away from this 2,000-square-foot shop.

Schwartz and the other sales associates here counsel brides and grooms on what to buy first when registering for china. "Most people list everything that's available," he explains, "but if you get a gravy boat and a coffee pot and only four place settings, what good does it do you?" Schwartz helps couples prioritize their wish lists so that their guests will understand that they prefer to receive all their place settings before any accessories. He does the same with stemware. "First thing you want are goblets and wine-glasses," he adds.

The sales staff can also guide you in matching stemware and flatware with your china pattern, which Schwartz calls tabletop coordination and design. "For example, if you pick a floral china, would you want to put a crystal with a geometric pattern with that? No, instead you should use a floral-style crystal," he says. To help customers understand this coordination concept, the store gives all registered couples A Guide to Tabletop Design, a booklet printed exclusively for Nat Schwartz & Co. In it are many of the tabletop coordination concepts couples discuss with the bridal consultants. But in addition to printed explanations, there are pages and pages of photographs of prematched china, crystal, and flatware so you can see exactly how this coordination system works.

You get the sense that the bridal consultants here are really looking out for your best interest. One bride had her heart set on registering for sterling silver flatware because she loved the way it looked. But a place setting was outrageously expensive, and the bride realized that the price might preclude any of her guests from getting her what she wanted. She discussed this fear with a consultant, who suggested she switch to a lower-priced yet still high-quality silver-plated setting. She did, and she received all eight place settings. Schwartz says he never has any qualms about talking someone out of an expensive setting. "I'll say, 'Here's a similar pattern for 50 percent less.'" Another customer wanted to register for French china. "I showed her how to save $200 by registering for an English pattern instead," he recalls.

Nat Schwartz & Co.'s prices are pretty competitive to begin with, so these cost-saving techniques can really save your guests some big bucks and ensure that you'll get just about everything you register for. The company says that it can offer such great prices for a simple reason: it buys stock in large quantities when manufacturers are running specials. This also helps prevent the need for items to be put on back order, since the company has a well-stocked warehouse.

You should have no trouble finding a pattern you like here; the company carries about 5,000 different patterns from manufacturers in America, France, Germany, England, Japan, and even Sri Lanka. Once your registry is completed, either in person or over the phone, the shop will mail you three copies of your registry list, registry cards to enclose with shower invitations, and as many copies of the catalog as you think you might need. Your guests can also call (800) 526-1440 to request a catalog. This is the same number they can use to purchase gifts, which will be wrapped for free. All returns are for store credit, unless a guest OKs a cash refund.

You and your guests can call (800) 526-1440 during normal business hours, which are Monday through Wednesday from 10:00 A.M. to 6:00 P.M., Thursday from 10:00 A.M. to 8:00 P.M., Friday from 10:00 A.M. to 6:00 P.M., and Saturday from 10:00 A.M. to 5:00 P.M. eastern time.

PACIFIC LINEN   ☛ *Bath and Bedding*

ROSS-SIMONS
9 Ross-Simons Drive   (800) 822-7433
(corporate headquarters)
Cranston, RI 02920

This discount cataloger headquartered in Rhode Island offers an extensive selection of china, crystal, and silver patterns from such well-known makers as Lenox, Mikasa, Royal Doulton, Noritake, Reed & Barton, and Oneida. The catalog from which you choose your patterns offers clear color pictures of the nearly 200 hundred designs available, and that's just in china alone. The company claims to have prices that are 20 to 70 percent below retail, and from what couples who've registered here have discovered, that information is about right on the money.

Registering here is simple—you can do it all over the phone. You'll be asked to estimate how many place settings you'd like to receive. That way Ross-Simons can check to see that your pattern isn't being discontinued and to make sure they have enough of your pattern in stock when the calls start coming in. However, should guests buy only a portion of the place settings, you are under no obligation to purchase the remaining sets. As soon as your registry is put on file, you'll be sent a printout of your selections as well as 40 or so registry cards that you can distribute to friends and family.

Ross-Simons doesn't keep its registry on-line, but it does update each registry every 24 hours. The company will gladly send catalogs to your guests to help them in purchasing your gifts. It will keep your registry on file for up to a year after your wedding to facilitate any additional gift purchases. Guests can also access your registry by visiting one of the Ross-Simons stores in Georgia, Maine, Nevada, and Rhode Island. Ross-Simons handles all returns the same way—you'll be issued a gift certificate that you can use to purchase something else from the catalog.

Operators on the registry line, (800) 82-BRIDE, are available Monday through Friday from 9:00 A.M. to 10:00 P.M., Saturday from 9:00 A.M. to 6:00 P.M., and Sunday from 11:00 to 6:00 P.M. eastern time.

SHREVE, CRUMP & LOW

330 Boylston Street   (617) 267-9100
(flagship store)   (800) 225-7088
Boston, MA 02116

👫

Since it began offering a bridal registry in 1933,
Shreve, Crump & Low has been synonymous with
Boston society. That is, almost as soon as her
fiancé slipped the diamond on her finger, a Boston
woman made an appointment to register her preferences at Shreve, Crump & Low. Today, the
wealthy in Boston still register here, but thankfully so do everyday couples, who are drawn to
the art deco–inspired store on Boylston Street
because of the great selection of china.

You can register at the Back Bay location
on Boylston Street or at the 6,200-square-foot
shop at the Chestnut Hill Mall location. Both
offer more than 400 china and flatware patterns
and more than 75 crystal designs, all from the
world's finest makers, like Herend, Limoges, and
Royal Copenhagen. Each store is luxuriously
appointed with inlaid mahogany cases and silver
leaf ceilings.

Shreve, Crump & Low, which celebrates its
200th anniversary in 1996, is one of those stores
where the registering couple is catered to like
royalty. A bridal consultant walks you around the
store helping you pick out china, crystal, and
silver and then writes everything down for you on
one of the store's registry forms. Really, all you
have to do to register is show up and point at and
nod to items you like. Once your wish list is
complete, a copy is sent to the other location so
they'll have your registry information on file as
well. Your guests can visit one of the Shreve,

Crump & Low shops or call (800) 225-7088 to make a purchase.

Before any piece of silver leaves Shreve's glass-topped cases, it is polished and placed in a felt bag to protect it on its journey. Another special touch the store offers: when you register for eight place settings and seven are purchased, the shop gives you the final place setting for free.

Your guest can call (800) 225-7088 Monday through Saturday from 9:30 A.M. to 5:30 P.M. eastern time. Store hours vary by location.

WATERFORD WEDGEWOOD
713 Madison Avenue   (800) 677-7860
(flagship store)
New York, NY 10021
🚶 ⬜

Most people think of Waterford and Wedgewood as simply manufacturers of crystal stemware and bowls and of china patterns. But the Irish company Waterford Wedgewood has a retail division with 10 locations in the United States, 8 of them offering bridal registries. Cities where these stores are located include Atlanta; Chicago; Honolulu; New York City; Santa Barbara, California; Santa Clara, California; Stamford, Connecticut; and St. Louis. (The outlet stores in Kittery, Maine, and Flemington, New Jersey, do not offer a registry.)

One of the benefits of registering here is the Waterford Wedgewood shops often carry hard-to-get items that would take department stores months to special order. Plus, prices sometimes are cheaper than what you would find elsewhere. Because you never know what's going to be in stock, it's best to register in person. Brides have requested a full set of china (not surprisingly) as well as table linens, crystal chandeliers and lamps, Christmas ornaments, and Reed & Barton stainless steel and sterling flatware.

Since each store's registry is not connected to the others by a computer system, when you register, you'll need to request that a copy of your list be sent to the stores where you think your guests might shop. Then your guests can call (800) 677-7860, and they will be automatically connected with the store nearest them to make purchases over the phone. All Waterford Wedgewood shops offer free gift wrapping and shipping for items purchased from a registry.

The stores try extremely hard to keep their bridal registries up-to-date to keep you from receiving duplicates. But, if you do, you can return anything to exchange it for something else at the store.

Your guests can call (800) 677-7860 Monday through Saturday from 10:00 A.M. to 6:00 P.M. local time. Store hours vary by location.

WILLIAM GLEN

2651 El Paseo Lane   (916) 485-3000
Sacramento, CA 95821   (800) 842-3322

The bridal consultants at William Glen prefer that you register in person. "Each china and crystal company has a different way of describing things, so we want to make sure you understand what you're registering for," explains consultant Nancy Keithley. The store does big business in Lenox, Noritake, and Wedgewood, and sales of Nambe silver trays and Wilton Armetale products are picking up as well.

If you're going to just register for china, silver, and crystal, you'll need to set aside about 45 minutes. However, if you're going to include the entire store—and you should, especially if you love to cook—then you'll need to set aside about two hours.

William Glen has an incredible selection of cookware and everyday kitchen items. The store carries a wide variety of items from Zyliss, a Swiss maker of gadgets, like a vegetable slicer, cheese grater, and garlic press, and many different kinds of Kitchen Source cutlery. Krups coffee-makers and espresso machines seem to pop up on a lot of registries as do bread machines and pasta makers.

Many guests prefer to shop via William Glen's toll-free number, (800) 842-3322. "When a guest calls in, we pull the registry in front of us and read the information," explains Keithley. Then, she'll ask the amount the guest wants to spend, take the guest's phone number, hang up, and then do some personal shopping for that person. Once she finds a selection of things she thinks the guest will like, she calls him or her back. "If the gift is sent within 100 miles of our store, the shipping is free," she adds.

The store asks that you call whenever you receive items on your registry list from another store. However, if you don't and you get duplicate gifts, William Glen will take returns in exchange for store credit.

Your guests can call (800) 842-3322 Monday through Friday from 9:30 A.M. to 6:00 P.M. Store hours are Monday through Thursday from 9:30 A.M. to 6:00 P.M., Friday from 9:30 A.M. to 9:00 P.M., Saturday from 9:30 A.M. to 5:30 P.M., and Sunday, 11:00 A.M. to 5:00 P.M. pacific time.

Home Decor

How you decorate your house says a lot about
your personality. When it comes to registering for
home furnishings, you needn't rely on department
stores alone anymore. A terrific option for those
with eclectic tastes is registering at a specialty
home decor store, and stores selling everything
from antiques to country-inspired furniture can
now help you with your registry needs. Many of
the stores listed in this section are managed by
the owners, which means you can expect
extremely personalized service.

There is one caveat to registering at this kind
of store: unique furnishings are just that—often
one of a kind. By registering at a store that
doesn't carry mass-produced items, you take a
chance that by the time your guests get around to
buying you your gift, it may be gone.

**ABC Carpet and
Home**

☛ *Bath and Bedding*

**Bed, Bath &
Beyond**

☛ *Bath and Bedding*

Bering's

☛ *Fine China and
Crystal*

C'est la Vie

☛ *The Whole Kitchen
Kaboodle*

City and Country

☛ *The Whole Kitchen
Kaboodle*

**The Container
Store**

☛ *Home Improvement*

CRATE & BARREL   ☛ *The Whole Kitchen Kaboodle*

DONECKERS   ☛ *Fine China and Crystal*

EDDIE BAUER HOME COLLECTION   ☛ *The Whole Kitchen Kaboodle*

FELISSIMO
10 West 56th Street
New York, NY 10019

(212) 247-5656
FAX: (212) 956-0081
FAX: (212) 956-3955

Even though you have the option of registering at Felissimo from afar, you really ought to visit this four-story, turn-of-the-century townhouse in Midtown Manhattan. Once inside, you'll have a hard time believing you're in the middle of New York City. That's because each floor is warmly decorated with all the store's wares, making you feel as if you've just walked into someone's home. You can register for anything in the store.

It makes perfect sense that the first floor is coined The Garden. Here, you'll find wind chimes, birdhouses, flower boxes, and bonsai garden fountains, one of the more popular items on Felissimo wish lists. On the second floor is a fully appointed bedroom and bathroom featuring handmade linens, plush goose down comforters, soaps, and lingerie. If you so choose, you can even add the wrought iron bed on display by San Francisco artist Eric Powell to your registry list. Upstairs on the third floor is the living room, which is furnished with overstuffed pillows, lighting fixtures, and handcrafted furniture. The dining room next door features handthrown dishes, Annie Glass serving platters along with out-of-the-ordinary sterling silver flatware, and dining room tables and chairs designed by a variety of American artists. The fourth floor is called Artspace and is actually a café where you can go for a cup of tea and a scone to relax after registering.

Felissimo is used to working with out-of-town couples who, not surprisingly, have friends and family living in faraway places. To make sure everyone on your guest list can access your registry, Felissimo will mail a copy of your wish list to whomever requests it, and a salesperson will even include Polaroid pictures of your requested items so guests can see what they're buying before they pay for it. All gift items can be shipped via UPS.

Felissimo is the kind of store that believes it is important to give back to the community. To that end, it pledges to donate a percentage of all registry purchases to the *New York Times* Neediest Cases Fund, which distributes contributions to seven New York–based charities.

Felissimo is open Monday through Saturday from 10:00 A.M. to 6:00 P.M. eastern time. On Thursdays, the store stays open until 8:00 P.M.

FROST & BUDD LTD.	☛ *Home Improvement*
GUMP'S	☛ *Fine China and Crystal*
THE HAY LOFT SHOPS	☛ *Fine China and Crystal*
HOMEPLACE	☛ *Bath and Bedding*

HOYA CRYSTAL GALLERY	☛ *Fine China and Crystal*
LAURA ASHLEY	☛ *Bath and Bedding*
L.L. BEAN	☛ *Sporting Goods*
LOWE'S HOME CENTERS	☛ *Home Improvement*

METROPOLITAN MUSEUM OF ART SHOPS

1000 Fifth Avenue,   (212) 650-2909
Mezzanine Gallery
(flagship store)
New York, NY 10028

Many of the couples who register at the Metropolitan Museum of Art Shops are not traditional
in any sense, explains Judy Block, a manager at the
New York shop. "They don't want china, glass,
and silver; instead, they want unusual things for
their home." And that's exactly what they'll find at
any of the 14 shops, located in New York City;
southern California; Denver; Connecticut; Atlanta;
New Jersey; Long Island, New York; Columbus,
Ohio; and Houston.

What makes owning items from the Metropolitan Museum of Art Shops so special is that
many of them are reproductions from actual
museum pieces. So you could register for hurri-
cane lamps in blue and mauve glass from the
Museum's American wing, terra-cotta lanterns
that an excavation team unearthed in eastern Iran
back in the 1930s, and a framed reproduction of
Vincent van Gogh's 1890 painting *Irises*.

Your wish list needn't be limited to furnishings. It can also include jewelry, note cards, books, serving dishes, plus china and crystal pieces that are reproductions inspired by the museum collection. For example, the Shops' "Tulips for the Table" place settings are reminiscent of Dutch painter Jacob Marrel's watercolor works of, what else?, tulips. Also on sale: reproductions of original Baroque Glasses crystal tumblers, traced back to Colonial New England, that appear in the Museum's American wing.

All you need to do to register is check in with Block at the mezzanine gallery at the shop in the main museum or her counterpart at one of the 13 other stores, get a form to fill out, and then simply walk around the shop writing down things you like. When you're done, the manager will add store sku numbers to your list and then keep it on file for when your guests come in. The shops' registry system is not computerized, so if your guests would like to shop at a location where you're not registered, they'll need to ask the manager to call the shop where your list is being held and have it faxed over. While the Metropolitan Museum of Art Shops offer a catalog, your guests cannot use it to buy gifts for you from your registry. But the individual shops can work with guests over the phone and then ship any purchases. The shops provide gift boxes and bows for free.

The shop at the main museum is open during museum hours, Tuesday through Thursday from 9:30 A.M. to 5:15 P.M., Friday and Saturday from 9:30 A.M. to 8:45 P.M., and Sunday from 9:30 A.M. to 5:15 P.M. eastern time. Hours at the other shops vary by location.

PACIFIC LINEN ☛ *Bath and Bedding*

RARITIES

7 East Superior Street   (312) 266-7777
Chicago, IL 60611

It didn't take store owner Gay Gelman long to decide to offer a bridal registry. "I remember when I got married and all the hideous gifts I got," she laughs. Gelman works hard to make sure her customers do not have the same experience. This store in downtown Chicago is filled with one-of-a kind objets d'art. Engaged couples can register for Romanian crystal, sterling silver vases, African masks, and pre-Columbian sculpture, to name a few items.

Gelman keeps the registry organized on the store's computer but she'll be very clear when she explains to you that because her store offers one-of-a-kind items, the articles on your registry list may be gone by the time your guests get you a gift. To avoid leaving your family and friends empty-handed, Gelman suggests you register for a large variety of items.

Rarities is a small, one-store operation, so Gelman isn't used to dealing with requests from out-of-towners. And because so much of the stock she carries is one-of-a-kind and delicate, she's very hesitant to ship items; she'd rather have guests visit the store, access the registry list, and make purchases in person.

Rarities is open seven days a week. Store hours are Monday through Friday from 12:00 noon to 5:00 P.M. and Saturday from 11:00 A.M. to 6:00 P.M. central time.

REAL GOODS TRADING CORPORATION   ☛ *Unconventional Items*

THE SEVENTH GENERATION CATALOG   ☛ *Bath and Bedding*

URBAN COUNTRY
7801 Woodmont Avenue   (301) 654-0500
Bethesda, MD 20814
👫

Urban Country prides itself on selling comfortable, overstuffed, soft furniture, including couches, armchairs, and beds, for every room of the house. Most of the items are sold under the Urban Country label and are probably unlike furnishings that you would find at a traditional furniture store. Urban Country also stocks knickknacks and decorating accessories, such as teapots and colorful serving platters, that its buyers pick up during shopping trips to Belgium, England, and Holland.

Jennifer Dauchess is the person to see when you decide to register, and she suggests that you make an appointment with her. This way, she can walk with you as you check out what Urban Country has to offer in this bilevel, 9,000-square-foot shop. When you see something you like, she'll write down your preferences for you.

This is the kind of store where there are many one-of-a-kind items. "I do let couples know that if they put one-of-a-kind items on their registry and they're gone, they can't be reordered," she explains. Oftentimes, she'll ask the registering couple to put second- and third-choice items on the registry in case something has been sold by the time their guests come into the store.

Guests can work with Dauchess over the phone or in person. Each gift purchased will be wrapped for free in an Urban Country box that is decorated with eucalyptus, baby's breath, raffia, and a ribbon. The store can take orders over the phone and ship items anywhere in the United States.

Urban Country is open Monday through Wednesday from 10:00 A.M. to 6:00 P.M., Thursday, 10:00 A.M. to 9:00 P.M., and Friday and Saturday from 10:00 A.M. to 6:00 P.M. eastern time.

WATERFORD ☞ *Fine China and*
WEDGEWOOD *Crystal*

YIELD HOUSE
P.O. Box 2525 (603) 356-2178
Conway, NH 03818-2525

Most people know Yield House as a catalog offering delightful country furniture at extraordinarily reasonable prices. But up in New Hampshire, in the land of outlet stores called North Conway, Yield House has a retail shop where you can register your gift preferences.

Most couples register for small pieces of furniture, like the Shaker-style end tables, Shaker-style hall table, and pinecone footstool. You can also request an armoire, a TV cupboard, and a dining room sideboard and hutch, along with throw pillows and quilts for your new bedroom. What's great about most of Yield House's furniture pieces is they can be ordered fully finished or in kit form—the latter can often chop up to 50 percent off the price—and you've got a choice of finishes. Some pieces can be done in painted, antique, or heirloom finish.

This registry is done through the retail store only, not through the mail-order division. Just walk around the store and write down the items you like. Your wish list will be placed in a three-ring binder covered in lovely green lace that is left out for guests to peruse when they come in to buy your gifts.

Even though the registry is based in the store, that doesn't preclude out-of-towners from registering here as well. Call the store and let them know you're interested in registering at Yield House, and someone will send you a registry form and a catalog, which you can use to select items. Once your list is complete, mail it back to the store, and it will be placed in that same green lacy binder with all the other wish lists.

Your guests can come to the store to access your registry, or they can call and work with a salesperson, who will look in the book, let them know the price ranges of wish list items, then take a credit card order, and ship the gift. Or a copy of your list along with a Yield House catalog will be sent to guests. They can buy something through the catalog, if they like. It's just real important that they call the store afterward and let a sales associate know what's been purchased so it can be crossed off the list.

Gift wrapping on all items is free. Anything that needs to be returned can be done for merchandise credit only.

Yield House is open Monday through Thursday from 10:00 A.M. to 5:00 P.M., Friday and

Saturday from 10:00 A.M. to 6:00 P.M., and Sunday from 12:00 noon to 5:00 P.M. eastern time.

Zona   ☛ *The Whole Kitchen Kaboodle*

Home Improvement

Maybe your new home is a "handyman's special." Or one of you is a Tim Allen wannabe. In any case, you'll be thankful to know that do-it-yourself shops, hardware stores, and even lumber yards let you register for gifts.

The experience of registering at one of these stores is worlds apart from registering anywhere else—a fact that becomes apparent the minute you walk in the door. Not only will you be faced with floor-to-ceiling shelves filled with wood and steel, but the salesperson who helps you may be wearing work boots and brushing sawdust off his or her sleeve while talking to you.

At many of these stores, the concept of having a bridal registry is a new one. Therefore, the process may seem primitive, and since many stores don't have their registries computerized yet, you could receive duplicate gifts. But rest assured—most home improvement stores have liberal return policies.

Ace Hardware
2710 20th Street   (815) 398-0111
(store with most extensive bridal registry)
Rockford, IL 61109
🚶 ☎

Each Ace Hardware store is individually owned

and operated, so it's completely up to the owner to decide if the store will offer a registry. In fact, the address and phone number listed here is for an Ace Hardware store that was one of the first to offer a registry program and normally works with other locations in helping them set up similar programs.

The person to talk to is Janice Westlund, who has been doing the registry at Bob's Ace Hardware in Rockford for 18 years and helps as many as 300 couples a year put together their wish lists. She can put you in touch with an Ace Hardware store near you that has a registry—currently, about 600 of the 5,000 Ace Hardware stores have them—or give you guidance on how you can convince your local Ace Hardware store to let you register there. If all else fails, Westlund can arrange it so that you can register at her store (even if you live out of town) and your guests can make all purchases over the phone.

While the merchandise at each store might vary slightly, here's what you can expect when registering at Ace Hardware. You can choose gifts for the yard, such as chain saws, grass trimmers, lawn mowers, rakes, shovels, and wheelbarrows; gifts for the bath, including hampers, scales, and soap dishes; gifts for the home, like fireplace equipment, humidifiers, and ceiling fans; gifts for entertaining, including gas grills and picnic baskets; gifts for the kitchen, such as juicers, popcorn makers, woks, cutlery, and barware; and gifts for the workshop, which guys seem to love and include power tools, glue guns, and hammers.

Your registry list, which is usually hand-written, is kept in a three-ring binder in the manager's office or at the customer service desk. Your guests can get a copy of the list when they visit the store. Most Ace Hardware stores can also work with guests over the phone to help them purchase gifts and have items shipped. Some stores even offer free gift wrapping and complimentary local delivery. Westlund's store keeps registry information on file up to 10 years and finds that many guests return to it again and again when buying anniversary or holiday gifts.

Ace Hardware store hours vary by location.

BERING'S ☞ *Fine China and Crystal*

BLACKHAWK HARDWARE ☞ *The Whole Kitchen Kaboodle*

BUILDERS SQUARE
9725 Datapoint Drive (corporate headquarters) San Antonio, TX 78229 (800) 338-NEWS

🚶🚶

What's great about being able to register at a place like Builders Square is it might actually inspire both bride and groom to get involved, especially when they see the variety of items that can appear on their registry list. It's only fair to let everyone in on the fun, since a wedding is indeed a joint effort. Builders Square, with stores in 21 states and Puerto Rico, has made the registry process as easy as possible.

Each store is mammoth, covering approximately 110,000 square feet, including 30,000 to 40,000 square feet devoted solely to gardening items. Because the task of walking up and down all those aisles might seem daunting, the store has devised a computerized version of the floor plan that lets you see what's available in each department, like hardware, lighting and lumber, without leaving the comfort of the customer service desk.

While the registry here isn't computerized, all 172 stores keep your registry on hand in a three-ring binder that is available through customer service, and they fax information back and forth between stores when necessary. If, for example, you register at the San Antonio store and you have friends in Syracuse who want to buy you a gift, the Syracuse store will call the one in San Antonio, ask them to fax a copy of your list to the store, and then call the San Antonio store back with a record of the purchases that have been made.

Store hours vary by location. You and your guests can get registry information by calling (800) 338-NEWS Monday through Friday from 9:00 A.M. to 5:00 P.M. central time.

THE CONTAINER STORE

13405 North Stemmons   (800)733-3532
    Freeway
(corporate headquarters)
Dallas, TX 75234-5767
🚶 🖥️

The Dallas-based Container Store sells thousands of different organizational and storage products for getting kitchens, bathrooms, closets, and home offices efficiently arranged. One of the store's bestsellers is the Elfa storage system, a series of white, plastic-covered wire baskets that you've probably seen many times in the homes of the extremely organized.

Registering at The Container Store makes perfect sense if you're moving into a home without a lot of closet space—specialists at the store will help you discover the best ways to get the most out of your small closets—or if you and your future spouse are merging two households and need some help in organizing your stuff.

You can register at any of the 14 stores in Georgia, Illinois, Maryland, Texas, and Virginia. The whole process has been made easier thanks to the store's lighthearted gift registry kit, which explains why registering here makes sense: "Across America, wedding gifts of all kinds are quietly being tucked away in dark attic corners, only to be dusted off and displayed when the giver pays a visit." While registering here may not totally curtail your receiving unneeded gifts, at least you'll have a place to efficiently store them.

The kit comes with a checklist of store items to help you formulate your wish list. You can choose from the following categories: kitchen/pantry, bath and laundry, closet, shelving/lifestyle, travel, and home office.

Once your registry list is handed to a salesperson, it takes about 24 hours for your registry to be on-line. Loved ones can access your list in two ways: 1) by visiting the store nearest them or 2) by calling the 800 number, using a credit card to purchase the gift, and having it shipped directly to you. The store promises to update your list every 24 hours to avoid your receiving duplicate gifts. If you change your mind and want to add something to your registry once it's up and running, you can simply call it in. But, they do request that you have the sku number ready to make things easier. And after your wedding day has come and gone, you're free to return any gift to one of the stores in exchange for another product or a store credit.

Operators at (800) 733-3532 are standing by Monday through Friday from 8:00 A.M. to 6:00 P.M. central time.

FROST & BUDD LTD.

750 East Lake Street   (612) 473-1442
Wayzata, MN 55391

🚶 💻

Engaged couples living in the Twin Cities area who happen to be building a home or moving into a new house after their wedding flock to Frost & Budd because of its extensive selection of outdoor items that are perfect for improving a lawn and garden. Here, these green-thumbed brides and grooms can register for everything from sundials to patio furniture to stone cherubs and gargoyles to line a garden walk. Many brides having a garden shower, which seems to be popular in the Midwest, can choose outdoor thermometers, green Wellington boots for wading in the mud, terra-cotta planting pots, and birdhouses.

From the outside Frost & Budd looks a lot like an old-time general store. Like a general store, it stocks a range of products. Besides gardening items, there's everyday china, glassware, lamps, dining room tables, and chairs. Surprisingly, the store's selection is more upscale and creative than its exterior would lead you to believe. For example, one of the most popular items on its registry is Salt Marsh pottery, hand-made in Cape Cod. These platters, dishes, and vessels are unique because the artist presses wild-flowers into the clay before firing and shaping them.

You decide how you'd like to design your
registry list here. You can choose items from
every category in the store or just limit your selection to one or two. You're free to walk around
at your own pace with or without the help of a
sales associate, select the wares you'd like to receive, and jot them down on one of Frost &
Budd's preprinted registry forms. Then everything is entered into the store's computers. If you
can't get to the store during regular business
hours because of a crazy work schedule, Frost &
Budd will even open the store up for you after
hours so you can register when it's convenient
(and less hectic) for you. Of course, you need to
call ahead and make an appointment for this
special arrangement.

If you've got guests living outside the Twin
Cities area, someone from Frost & Budd will
gladly fax or mail your registry list to them. Or
the store will work with them over the phone in
describing what's on your wish list, finding out
how much your guests want to spend, taking a
credit card order, and arranging for the gift to be
shipped out.

Frost & Budd is open Monday through
Saturday from 9:30 A.M. to 6:00 P.M. central time.

HOME DEPOT
2727 Paces Ferry Road, N.W   (404) 433-8211
(corporate headquarters)
Atlanta, GA 30339
🚶 🖥️

The first stop you'll need to make when you go
to register at Home Depot is the special services
desk. There, you can hook up with a salesperson
who can accompany you around the store and
help you complete your wish list. Or, if you're

a tried-and-true Home Depot customer (as many fellas seem to be these days) and you've already jotted down what you'd like included on your registry list, you can drop that list off at the special services desk. "We leave it up to our customers on how they want to register," says Tammy Erebia, a manager in the Pontiac, Michigan, store.

No matter which way you choose to register, your information is entered in Home Depot's computerized system and available within a business day at all 355 Home Depot stores in 28 states and three Canadian provinces.

Your guests will need to stop by the special services desk so they can pick up a copy of your list. Or, if they can't get to a Home Depot store, they can call any location and ask that your list be read over the phone. Guests can make purchases over the phone and have items shipped—within reason. Some of the larger items in the store, like Jacuzzis and lumber, will need to be picked up. Anything that is purchased for you can be returned to any Home Depot location to be exchanged or for cash back.

Here are the Home Depot departments from which you can choose wish-list items: building materials, lumber, floor and wall, paint, hardware, plumbing, electrical, garden, ceiling fans, lighting and specialty areas, design center, and kitchen cabinet area. One bride and groom who were redoing their backyard registered for plants, bushes, and various landscaping materials. Another couple, who was updating their home's bathroom, requested a tub and a medicine cabinet.

Store hours vary by Home Depot location.

HQ

575 Lynnhaven Parkway   (804) 498-7100
(corporate headquarters)
Virginia Beach, VA 23452 (800) 621-7882

🚶

With more than 40,000 items in stock in its warehouse-sized stores, HQ (Home Quarters Warehouse, Inc.) offers every home improvement item
that newlyweds could want. Popular registry items
include ceiling fans, gas and electric grills, Honey-
well security systems, and Rubbermaid lawn and
deck furniture. If you happen to be building a
deck at your new home, you and your fiancé can
also register for lumber and hardware, and HQ's
computers can help you design the deck right in
the store.

Because HQ stores are so big, it makes sense
to work with a sales associate when you go to
register. He or she can talk to you about the kinds
of things you'd like to add to your wish list and
then escort you to the areas where you'll find
those items. (Otherwise, you could get lost
wandering up and down the mammoth aisles.)
Once there, for each item you'll be asked to jot
down the item name, a brief description of the
item, and the sku number on a preprinted form.
When your list is completed, it will be placed in a
bridal registry book, which is held at the customer
service desk.

Unfortunately, each HQ has a separate
registry book, and the store does not keep registry
information on a centralized computer system.
But you have a number of options for getting
your registry information to guests who don't
live near the store where you've registered. You

can copy your list and give it to your maid of
honor to distribute. You can ask the store to
fax your list to other HQ locations where you
know your friends and family will be shopping.
Or your guests can call the HQ store with your
list on file and ask that it be faxed or mailed to
them. Your guests can also purchase items by mail
order, although there are certain registry items
that HQ cannot ship, such as plants and hot tubs.

HQ understands that its registry program is
not foolproof and therefore offers a no-questions-
asked return policy. You can bring duplicate items
back to any one of HQ's 50 stores, all of which
are located east of the Mississippi River, for a
store credit or cash refund.

Store hours vary by location.

Knobs 'n Knockers
Peddler's Village   (215) 794-8045
P.O. Box 459
Lahaska, PA 18931

This upscale hardware store in Bucks County,
Pennsylvania, attracts a variety of different
couples to its registry program. "We get a lot of
people who are out here from Philadelphia or
New York City, and they may be refurbishing an
apartment or an off-time retreat," says Phyllis, the
store's bridal consultant. "Or, they're getting
married for a second time. They probably already
have a home or apartment, so they're looking for
very specific things, not just any toaster."

"What couples who register here are typically
looking for is a fireplace ensemble," she continues,
"or bathroom accessories. Or maybe they're reno-
vating some furniture that their grandmother gave
them, and they want to update it with new knobs."

Just as its names typifies, you can register at Knobs 'n Knockers for all kinds of knobs—door knobs and knobs to put on furniture—and knockers as well. The store also stocks brass nameplates for the front door, lamps to illuminate your front porch, and racks to hang towels on in the bathroom, among other accessories to improve the look of your home.

When you register here, "I'll find out what color scheme you're interested in or what period furniture or type of house you have," Phyllis explains. Then, she will walk you around the store or let you peruse it on your own and jot down the things you like on a preprinted registry sheet that breaks out the store's items by category. When completed, your registry will be entered in the store's computer system.

Because Knobs 'n Knockers is located in such a remote place, the store is used to working with out-of-town guests who call to access registries and purchase gifts. A salesperson will describe items on your list over the phone and, if necessary, send guests Polaroid pictures of the merchandise.

Knobs 'n Knockers is open Monday through Thursday from 10:00 A.M. to 5:30 P.M., Friday and Saturday from 10:00 A.M. to 9:00 P.M., and Sunday from 11:00 A.M. to 5:30 P.M. eastern time.

LOWE'S HOME CENTERS

Customer Relations   (910) 651-4000
    Department   (800) 44-LOWES
(corporate headquarters)
Box 1111
North Wilkesboro, NC 28656-0001
👫

Back in 1946, Lowe's Home Centers started as a

single hardware store in North Wilkesboro, North Carolina, owned and operated by James Lowe. Ten years later, his brother-in-law H. Carl Buchan bought the store with the dream of creating a chain of hardware stores that would buy directly from manufacturers and then be able to offer customers merchandise at a discount. Well, Buchan's dream has come true. Today there are 344 Lowe's Home Centers in 22 states, each offering anywhere from 14,000 to 40,000 items at everyday low prices, which are guaranteed. "If you find an identical item in stock at another retailer in the market at a lower price, we will match that price plus take 10 percent off," explains Cinny Haynes, a company spokesperson.

Lowe's is just entering the bridal registry market, so not all of its 100,000-square-foot-plus stores offer a full-fledged program yet, and the services at the participating stores vary. But, a call to Lowe's store locator number, (800) 44-LOWES, will help you track down a store in your area where you can register.

Do-it-yourselfers are going to love this store, especially Tool World, the department where you'll find a huge, hands-on selection of power tools and equipment by Black & Decker and Stanley, just to name a couple of manufacturers. Some customers have dubbed this area of the store "handyman heaven."

The lawn and garden area, for example, includes a 6,000-square-foot greenhouse with a year-round selection of tropical and exotic plants. Couples have been known to register for the large trees on display here as well as fountains and stat-uaries. Over in the bath department, you can add a tub and toilet to your wish list or keep things a bit smaller and ask for area mats, a sink, or a faucet. The Lowe's home office center stocks Compaq and Packard Bell computers plus printers, faxes, modems, and 160 different software packages. You can check out ready-to-assemble furniture (bookcases, desks, entertainment centers, and so forth) in the furnishings area.

Each Lowe's store also offers free computerized kitchen planning services and paint color matching. If you've got a specific home improvement project in mind, such as redesigning your kitchen or painting your house, you can take advantage of these services and then register for all the products that will allow you to finish the project.

You and your guests can call (800) 44-LOWES Monday through Friday from 9:00 A.M. to 5:00 P.M. eastern time. Store hours vary by location.

MERRIFIELD GARDEN CENTER

8132 Lee Highway   (703) 560-6222
P.O. Box 848
(flagship store)
Merrifield, VA 22116

"People register here because of our large selection of plants," says Julie Guy, a company spokesperson. "A lot of people tend to be getting married later or are having second weddings, and they have all the china they need. So if they're moving to a new home, they come to us for our selection of outdoor and indoor plants." In fact, the most popular trees on Merrifield's registries are dogwood, crape myrtle (a flowering shrub), and weeping cherries.

Those who register at one of the two Merrifield locations don't necessarily stop at trees when it comes to requesting items to decorate their yard. They also register for statuaries, gardening accessories, fish to put in outdoor ponds, vases, and pots. At the Fairfax, Virginia, store, a 10,000-square-foot greenhouse is home to a large selection of annuals and perennials as well. "People have also registered for a landscape design that's being done at their house," adds Guy, "and guests who come in can contribute funds to that project."

Because it's best to see certain plants before you buy them, you are encouraged to register in person. The store gives you a registry sheet to fill out, which is just one page and very basic. It covers only three areas: the greenhouse, the dried flowers department, and the garden shop (where you'll find seeds, wind chimes, and bird feeding supplies). Anything you want that doesn't fall into one of these three areas can be added on the back of the sheet.

When you register at the Merrifield location, your list is automatically faxed to the Fairfax store, and vice versa. This way, guests can visit either store. Or they can call one of the stores and work with a salesperson over the phone. "I always find out the dollar value they want to spend," says Guy, "and whether they want us to deliver the gift." Most potted plants and trees are automatically delivered to the gift recipient's house, and guests usually spring for the installation cost of planting the tree as well.

Store hours at both Merrifield Garden Centers fluctuate according to the season.

REAL GOODS TRADING CORPORATION   ☛ *Unconventional Items*

Zarsky Lumber Company, Inc.

P.O. Box 2527   (512) 573-2479
(flagship store)   (800) 622-0604
Victoria, TX 77902

🚶

Even though Zarsky Lumber Company has locations in seven Texas cities—Corpus Christi,
Harlingen, McAllen, Refugio, Rio Grande City,
Victoria, and Wharton   only the Victoria store
currently offers a registry program. "However, if
someone lived in one of the other cities, they
could probably figure out a way to set up the
registry," says Cally Coleman Hargraves, the
brainchild behind Zarsky Lumber Company's
registry program, in place since 1993. "Likewise,
if guests lived in other cities, the Victoria store
would work with the other stores in getting them
the registry list and helping the guest buy gifts."

Hargraves is the person to contact if you're
interested in registering at Zarsky Lumber
Company. She was actually the store's first bride
to register, convincing her father, the store's
owner, there was need for such a registry. "I
picked out a water hose, a rake, and paintbrushes.
My husband chose tools," she says. At first, she
thought that most of the people who would
register at Zarsky Lumber Company would be
older couples, but she was wrong. "A lot of people
are throwing home improvement showers, where
it's a couple's shower, so it's very practical," she
says. "Or the couples who register here have
bought an old home, and they need to fix it up."
Many of these couples have been apartment
dwellers all their adult lives, so they request things
that used to come automatically with their apartment, like trash cans, fire extinguishers, and
smoke detectors.

Either Hargraves or another employee will walk with you around the store and help you pick out items to include on your wish list. The categories from which you can choose are lawn and garden, power tools, hand tools, gifts for the home, plumbing, and other—that might mean an ice chest or a stepladder, items that don't easily fit into specific categories.

As mentioned earlier, Zarsky Lumber Company will work with out-of-town guests in getting them a copy of your wish list and, if necessary, helping them select a gift over the phone (they can call on the store's toll-free number), pay for it by credit card, and then have it delivered. "I usually wrap and deliver gifts to people myself," says Hargraves. Her gift wrap of choice? Brown paper and twine. "It's appropriate, because we are a hardware store," she adds with a smile.

Returns are never a problem, because the store includes a receipt (without the price on it, of course) with all gift purchases. Items can be returned for store credit or cash.

The Zarsky Lumber Company store in Victoria is open Monday through Friday from 7:30 A.M. to 5:00 P.M. and Saturday from 7:30 A.M. to 3:00 P.M. central time.

Honeymoon

Perhaps you and your fiancé believe you truly have everything you could possibly need and that registering just doesn't make sense. Or a romantic Caribbean getaway, something you've dreamed about all your life, seems beyond your bank account. Well, there's good news. You can now register for a honeymoon.

Since a honeymoon is something every newly married couple is expected to take, don't feel guilty about registering for one. Your guests expect that you'll register *somewhere* and will want to buy you a gift that you'll truly use and enjoy. So, why not check out the four companies listed below that can help you arrange a dream honeymoon—one that you won't have to pick up the tab for. Bon voyage!

AMBASSADOR TRAVEL AGENCY INC.

2474 North George Street   (800) 296-9019
York, Pennsylvania 17402

It usually takes Carol Walker, owner of Ambassador Travel Agency, three meetings with a couple to figure out their ideal honeymoon, especially if they don't have any ideas about places they'd like to visit for this special trip. "First I find out about them and their interests, a budget they want to work with, and then I give them information on different destinations," she says. At the second meeting, she'll help the couple narrow down choices. "After they've looked at six or seven places in the Caribbean, for example, they might say, 'We like St. Lucia, St. Kitts, or St. Thomas,'" she adds. Then, on the third meeting, they finalize everything.

You don't have to visit Walker's agency in person to register here—she's happy to work with you over the phone.

The agency doesn't currently have any registry cards that couples can enclose in invitations, but many of the couples who've registered with Ambassador slip a note into their shower invitation listing the agency's toll-free number. Guests who want to contribute to a couple's registry must send a check; Walker doesn't accept credit cards for registry donations. In return, she'll send them a linen-embossed card with their name and amount donated printed on the card that they can give in lieu of a wedding gift at the actual affair. Or, if a guest requests, the card can be sent directly to the couple.

The only problem Walker runs into with the honeymoon registry is the fact that most trips must be paid in full about 30 days before the departure date, oftentimes before the wedding invitations have been mailed. "So couples end up putting the entire trip amount on their credit card," says Walker. Once all the funds have been collected from guests, she issues the couple a check so they can pay the credit card balance.

Most of the time guest contributions take care of a good portion of the trip. On rare occasions, the whole thing gets paid for. Walker recalls the couple who registered for a $3,000 honeymoon at Sandals St. Lucia. She adds, "They had the whole thing covered by their guests."

Ambassador Travel Agency is open Monday through Friday from 8:00 A.M. to 5:30 P.M. and Saturday from 9:00 A.M. to 1:00 P.M. eastern time.

BACKROADS
1516 Fifth Street   (800) 462-2848
Berkeley, CA 94710

Since so many newlyweds choose to go on a Backroads biking vacation for their honeymoon, the company reasoned that it made sense to offer a honeymoon registry, a program that has been in effect since November 1994.

If biking isn't your cup of tea, don't worry—Backroads isn't just about two-wheeled wonders. The company also offers walking and hiking, cross-country skiing, running, and multisport vacation packages, allowing you to take a honeymoon of choice at any time of the year.

At least six months before your departure date, call Backroads and ask to speak with someone about the honeymoon registry. At this time, you can request a catalog that lists all trips for the upcoming year. There are usually about 135 different itineraries to choose from. Backroads destinations range from France's Loire Valley to California's wine country to the Canadian Rockies, and all package prices include meals, accommodations (often at world-class inns), maps, van support, and more.

Once you've decided on a destination and a date, you'll be asked to leave a deposit—it's $300 for a domestic trip and $400 for an international excursion. Backroads doesn't have any registry cards to give you but will gladly send a letter to anyone on your guest list letting them know that you've registered with Backroads. Guests can use a check or credit card to apply funds to your registry account; a minimum payment of $25 is requested. Then a gift card is sent to you, saying "A donation has been given toward your honeymoon by [guest's name]. Have a wonderful trip."

About 30 days before you leave on your trip, Backroads will call you and let you know how much has been contributed so far. The company does this so that in case you need to pay for any outstanding amount for the trip, it doesn't come as a shock when the bill arrives. Two weeks later, you'll be asked to pay the balance in full if your guests haven't already taken care of that. If, after your honeymoon, you're curious to see which guests contributed how much to your trip, Backroads can provide you with such a printout.

You and your guests can call the Backroads toll-free line, (800) 462-2848, Monday through Friday from 8:30 A.M. to 5:30 P.M. pacific time.

CARLSON WAGONLIT TRAVEL
6178 Oxon Hill Road   (800) 232-6537
Suite 103
Oxon Hill, MD 20745
🚶 ☎

"One of our agents was getting married in 1994. While looking through the bridal magazines, she saw all of these ads for honeymoons. We began to think about how expensive it is planning a honeymoon as well as a wedding, so we came up with the idea of having a honeymoon registry," explains Terry Mooney, an agency manager. Since its inception in October 1994, Carlson Wagonlit Travel's honeymoon registry has been a smashing success. "Everyone who has used the service so far has had the entire honeymoon covered," he says.

When you register at this D.C.–area travel agency, Mooney opens an account for you through which he tracks the amount of money your guests contribute toward your preselected honeymoon. Guests send checks directly to the agency, and then they receive a gift certificate showing the amount they spent toward your trip that they can enclose in a wedding gift card.

Thirty days before you depart, the agency lets you know whether you've received enough money to cover the trip. "Then, before you actually leave, you'll come in and pay the remaining balance," says Mooney. Or, if the total funds that have been donated to your account exceeds the trip amount, Mooney will issue you a check for the extra amount or he'll upgrade your trip.

Most couples who register for the service do so as far as nine months in advance of their wedding, probably to ensure that guests invited to engagement parties and showers have ample time to access their registry. Mooney has no problem working with brides- and grooms-to-be who live beyond the Washington, D.C. city limits. They just call the agency's toll-free number, (800) 232-6537, and Mooney arranges everything over the phone.

Carlson Wagonlit Travel is open Monday through Friday from 9:00 A.M. to 5:30 P.M. and Saturday and Sunday from 12:00 noon to 4:00 P.M. eastern time.

ELLIOTT TRAVEL
Twelve Oaks Mall   (810) 348-3303
27542 Novi Road
(flagship location)
Novi, MI 48377
🚶 ☎

Unlike other travel agencies offering a honeymoon registry, Elliott Travel doesn't track the amount guests apply toward your honeymoon. Instead, guests call any of the eight Elliott Travel locations in Michigan (which are all connected by computer) and buy a gift certificate in any denomination they choose. Guests can present that gift certificate to you at your engagement party or shower or have it mailed directly to you. Once you've received all the certificates, you apply the total amount to your honeymoon package. (It's really important that you keep these certificates in a safe place so you don't lose them.)

Amy Ruffing, manager of two of the Elliott Travel locations, suggests that couples register for their honeymoon at least two months in advance of their wedding—or even earlier if they expect to have an engagement party and more than one bridal shower. "A honeymoon has to be paid for 30 days prior to departure," she explains. Any gift certificates that are purchased for you after that time can be redeemed at the agency either for cash or for an upgrade on your trip.

Elliott Travel will help you decide on a honeymoon destination in person or over the phone. Then, once you've decided on the trip you'd like to take, you'll be asked to leave a $100 deposit. "This will hold your reservation for up to a year," adds Ruffing. Information about your destination of choice, wedding date, and so on will be entered into Elliott's computer system immediately, so that agents at all eight offices can access it. Couples who've taken advantage of Elliott's registry have booked trips to Jamaica, Cancun, Grand Cayman, and Hawaii, and some have even gone on cruises.

Seven of the eight Elliott Travel agencies are located in malls, where office hours generally are Monday, Thursday, and Friday from 9:00 A.M. to 9:00 P.M., Tuesday and Wednesday from 9:00 A.M. to 6:00 P.M., Saturday from 10:00 A.M. to 6:00 P.M., and Sunday from 12:00 noon to 5:00 P.M. eastern time.

Sporting Goods

If you and your future spouse met on a sports team or while hiking in the mountains, the best registry for you two is the kind that allows you to register for gifts that let you continue your athletic pursuits together—namely, a sporting goods store or catalog. One couple who planned to spend their honeymoon backpacking in the mountains registered for everything they needed for that excursion, including sleeping bags and a portable stove.

The registry atmosphere at sporting goods stores is very relaxed. You'll probably be asked to take a look around the store, jot down your requests on a piece of paper, and hand it over. Like other specialty stores, here you'll find experienced salespeople—some who are athletes themselves—who can talk to you intelligently about your equipment needs and the various sporting goods available in the store. And, since they share a common interest with you, they can help make the registry process as worthwhile and enjoyable as possible.

BOAT/U.S. MARINE CENTERS
880 S. Pickett Street   (703) 461-2850
Alexandria, VA 22304
🚶🚶

While there are 33 BOAT/U.S. Marine Centers locations across the country, it's not a retail chain per se. Instead, it's the retail arm of BOAT/U.S., the Boat Owners Association of the United States, a veritable AAA for boat owners. The organization currently boasts a membership base of more than 500,000. Non–BOAT/U.S. members can shop and register for items at any of the retail locations, but members, who pay only $12.50 a year, are guaranteed discounts on the more than 4,000 boating items each store stocks.

Obviously, you'll want to be a boat owner, crew member, or nautical fanatic to join the association and register here. You can register for dinghies, dive equipment, compasses, and anchors. You'll also find products at the centers that can be used on a boat and off. For example, you can register for Melamine dishes, some with nautical designs and others that look like china. Sure, they won't break if they slide off the table in your boat, but they're also pretty enough to use around the house. Likewise, you can request cookbooks that are perfect for couples on the move. One, cleverly titled *Cooking on the Go*, by J. Groene (Hearst Books, 1987), applies to meals at a campsite equally as well as to meals made on a boat.

Each BOAT/U.S. Marine Centers location has ties to the other ones across the country, so if you register in one location, you can request to have your list faxed or called in to another one somewhere else. The centers are set up to take orders from guests over the phone and ship merchandise. Returns are accepted, no questions asked, for a replacement or refund.

For the location nearest you or to obtain membership information, call (800) 395-2628. BOAT/U.S. Marine Centers hours vary by location.

CAMPMOR

810 Route 17 North   (201) 445-5000
Paramus, NJ 07652   (800) CAMPMOR

🚶 ✉ 📠 📖

One couple who registered at Campmor did so because they were getting married in an outdoor ceremony on Mount Washington and spending their honeymoon camping in New Hampshire. "They registered for clothing, backpacks, North Face sleeping bags, sleeping pads, and a tent," recalls Barbara Strubberg, who runs Campmor's registry program.

The entire Campmor store in New Jersey plus the catalog is at your disposal when registering here. "If you're registering from the catalog, it's easier if you write down item numbers from the catalog," says Strubberg, who will send a registry form and a catalog to you if you're an out-of-towner who wants to register your wish list with this gigantic sporting goods store. Just call the store's toll-free line, (800) CAMPMOR, and ask for Strubberg. The catalog is nothing special to look at—it's printed on newspaper and includes line drawings of merchandise—but it's packed with 152 pages of great outdoor gear from 57 different categories, ranging from T-shirts to tents to Teva sandals.

If you'd like, Strubberg will send copies of your list and catalogs to your guests, or she'll fax them your list. "One couple asked that I mail a copy of the list and a catalog to all their guests, which I did," she says. She'll also personally gift wrap any smaller items that are purchased for you and ship them. The store can neither wrap nor ship bigger merchandise such as canoes and bikes—your guests will have to pick such items up or notify you that the items are waiting for you at the store.

Because Strubberg keeps a record of all purchases made from the registry, returns are never a problem. You can bring or mail something back in exchange for another item, store credit, or cash.

You and your guests can call (800) CAMPMOR, during store hours, which are Monday through Friday from 9:30 A.M. to 9:30 P.M. and Saturday from 9:30 A.M. to 6:00 P.M. eastern time.

EREHWON MOUNTAIN OUTFITTERS
2585 Waukegan Road   (708) 948-7250
(flagship store)
Bannockburn, IL 60015
🚶 ☎

The registry here is about as casual as a pair of
Birkenstock sandals. Just hand over a handwritten
list of the items you'd like to receive and, voilà,
you're registered. One couple decided to register
here because they were planning to spend their
honeymoon hiking in the mountains. What did
they ask for? A tent, sleeping bags, and a portable
stove.

There are four Erehwon Mountain Outfitters
stores in the Chicago area and one in Madison,
Wisconsin. The stores talk to each other all the
time. Therefore, there's no need to worry if
you've registered at a Chicago store but have
friends in Wisconsin. The store in Madison will
simply call the store where you've registered and
then relay your registry requests to the store in
Wisconsin.

Store hours vary by location.

LANDS' END   ☞ *Bath and Bedding*

L.L. BEAN
Casco Street   (800) 341-4341
Freeport, ME 04033   extension 3226
🚶 ✉ 📠 ☎ 💻 📖   FAX: (207) 878-8418

With an entire catalog dedicated to outdoor and
adventure gear and apparel, L.L. Bean is an ideal
place for an outdoorsy couple to register for their
wedding. And what's great is there's no need to
trek up to the Freeport, Maine, store—although
that's a fun road trip to take—to do it.

L.L. Bean offers you a multitude of registry choices. If you can get to the store, you can register there. Otherwise, call the registry hotline, (800) 341-4341 extension 3226, and request that a gift registry kit be sent to you. At that time, you'll be asked which L.L. Bean catalogs you would like enclosed. There are a handful of them to choose from besides the outdoors one. For example, there's the general clothing catalog, plus one dedicated to home and camp, which includes stoneware, stainless steel flatware, bedding, and furniture.

About 10 days later, the kit will arrive, jam-packed with the catalogs you requested, a cover letter than explains L.L. Bean's registry program, a worksheet on which to write down your prefer-ences, a sheet on which you can write the names and addresses of friends and family to whom you'd like L.L. Bean to mail a copy of your list and a catalog, and a gift registry suggestion list, just in case you have trouble deciding. Once you've completed the forms, you can call the information in to the registry hotline, mail it back in the postage-paid envelope that comes with your kit, or fax it to (207) 878-8418. As soon as L.L. Bean receives your wish list, a gift registry representa-tive will send you a confirmation letter along with a completed version of your list.

Because L.L. Bean keeps its registry informa-tion on a centralized computer system, your guests can access your list either at the retail store or via the toll-free number, and purchases made either way will be instantly recorded. This system helps to cut down on duplications. However, if you do need to return something, L.L. Bean stands behind its products 100 percent and will replace any item, offer you an exchange, credit a bank card, or refund the purchase. Last-minute shoppers will appreciate knowing that Federal Express delivery is available at no extra charge.

Some of the more popular items to register for from L.L. Bean are blueberry stoneware, flannel sheets, wool blankets, Adirondack chairs, and hammocks, plus all kinds of sporting gear, including dome tents, sleeping bags, and the weather station radio (so you won't get caught in a snowstorm when you're out hiking).

You can call L.L. Bean's Registry Hotline, (800) 341-4341 extension 3226, seven days a week from 8:00 A.M. to 10:00 P.M. eastern time. The L.L. Bean retail store is open 24 hours a day.

PARAGON SPORTING GOODS
867 Broadway   (212) 255-8036
New York, NY 10003

"Paragon Sporting Goods is a New York institution," says Dan Zadek, a Paragon Sporting Goods spokesperson, of the downtown store that's been around since 1908. "When you're looking for toys, you go to FAO Schwarz. When you want menswear, you go to Barneys. And when you want sporting goods, you come to us."

Since Paragon started its registry program in 1992, a number of couples have visited the store to register for gifts. "A couple who likes diving or snorkeling would focus on masks, fins, and wet suits," says Zadek. "A couple who likes to go camping would register for sleeping bags, expensive technical outdoor clothing, hiking boots, etcetera." Besides diving, snorkeling, and camping, you'll find equipment for many other sports on Paragon's three selling floors. "We think of ourselves as a series of specialty shops under one roof," he adds. There's clothing for sailing, tennis, aerobics, and skiing; tennis racquets; downhill and cross-country skis; in-line skates; bicycles; a full range of fitness equipment; sunglasses, and more. The two sports that Paragon doesn't touch on are bowling and hunting.

Registering here is really simple: just walk around the store and write down the items that you and your fiancé would like to receive. Then, that list is copied into Paragon's bridal registry book. When guests come into the store, they can take a copy of the list with them, or if they live outside New York City, the store will fax it to them and let them make purchases over the phone.

A bit of Paragon trivia: It is this store's exterior that is shown on TV's "Mad About You" as Buchman's Sporting Goods.

Paragon Sporting Goods is open Monday through Saturday from 10:00 A.M. to 8:00 P.M. and Sunday from 11:00 A.M. to 6:30 P.M. eastern time.

REAL GOODS TRADING CORPORATION

☞ *Unconventional Items*

RECREATIONAL EQUIPMENT INCORPORATED

P.O. Box 1700
Sumner, WA 98390-0900

(800) 828-5533
FAX: (206) 891-2523

🚶 ✉ 🖩 💻 📖

REI (Recreational Equipment Incorporated) was founded back in 1938 when a group of Pacific Northwest climbers realized that there weren't any stores around where they could obtain good climbing equipment. REI is actually a cooperative, since many of the people who shop here also pay dues to the company. For the $15 a year they spend, the 1,500,000 members of the REI cooperative share in company dividends, receive advanced notice of store sales, save money on travel with trips through REI Adventures, and get discounts on any labor charges they might incur in REI's ski and bike shops.

You don't have to be an REI member to register here—just a lover of outdoor sports. REI currently has nearly 45 store locations in 20 states, from as far west as Anchorage, Alaska, and back east as Reading, Massachusetts. Plus, there's a fully operational mail-order division, giving you the option of registering with REI even if you don't live near one of its stores. If this is the route you take, you can use REI's catalog as your guide, but keep in mind that the catalog doesn't carry nearly as much merchandise as the stores do.

You can select equipment from any of REI's departments—camping, climbing, paddling, clothing, footwear, skiing, and cycling. However, REI sells skiing and cycling merchandise only at the stores, not through the catalog, due to the fitting needs of customers.

Whether you register in person, by fax, or through the mail, you'll be asked to fill out one of REI's registry forms and then deliver it to the customer service department. Call (800) 828-5533 to request that registry information and a catalog be sent to you. Within 24 hours, your wish list will be entered into REI's computers and will be available at all stores plus through the catalog. Your guests can visit a store or call REI's mail-order department. However, guests who want to shop over the phone can do so only on weekdays, since REI's mail-order department is closed on weekends. When a purchase is made at a store, your registry is instantaneously updated—that is, it is if your guest remembers to bring the registry form back to the customer service department. Otherwise, it could take the store as long as 24 hours to update your registry. All mail-order purchases are recorded right away.

Like many sporting goods stores, REI sells its own line of equipment and clothing along with those from major manufacturers. Popular registry items hail from both and include REI's GeoDome tent, which can accommodate four to six people; Coleman stoves, which run on kerosene or white gas and heat up in just two minutes; filters of all kinds to purify any questionable water; and North Face's Blue Kazoo sleeping bag filled with goose down.

For out-of-town registries, call REI's mail-order department at (800) 828-5533 Monday through Friday from 7:00 A.M. to 5:00 P.M. pacific time. Most REI stores are open Monday through Friday from 10:00 A.M. to 9:00 P.M., Saturday, 10:00 A.M. to 6:00 P.M. and Sunday from 11:00 A.M. to 5:00 P.M. local time.

SPORT CHALET
920 Foothill Boulevard   (818) 790-9800
(flagship store)
La Canada, CA 91011
🚶🚶

Sport Chalet is a chain of 18 sporting goods stores in southern California. The couples who register here spend their weekends in-line skating at Venice Beach or hiking in the Sierra Nevada Mountains. "We attract those people who have been married once before or are very active sports enthusiasts," says Bob Houter, a company spokesperson.

You can register for anything that Sport

Chalet sells—ski equipment, camping products, fishing poles, bicycles, tennis racquets, and even baseball gloves. Since Sport Chalet certifies and trains divers, you can register for scuba equipment and lessons, too. "One couple registered for scuba lessons, and they got it," Houter recalls. The only sports-oriented merchandise that Sport Chalet doesn't carry is guns and ammunition.

Sport Chalet is primarily a retail location, so you'll need to register in person and your guests will have to visit one of the store locations to access your list and buy gifts. Sport Chalet does not ship items. Once your wish list is complete, a copy is sent to the corporate office, and then it is distributed to all store locations. The registry is not kept on-line, "but we try to keep it updated as best we can," says Houter. "But if we slip up, you can return anything for an exchange. We're very liberal."

Store hours vary by location.

Unconventional Items

Your friends and family might do a double take if you told them you'd registered for a home mortgage, for his-and-hers pajamas, or for a vintage bottle of wine. But when it comes to registering, anything is possible these days.

The benefit of registering for unconventional items is that you can get a theme thing going (like music or a mortgage) or you can give your guests more of a price option when shopping for gifts. When you register at an offbeat business, you can also expect individualized service, since many of them are single-location operations and there's a good chance that when you register you'll be dealing directly with the owner.

BANK AMERICA MORTGAGE
333 Earle Ovington Boulevard   (800) 272-6791
Uniondale, NY 11553

☎ ▢

It is in the game plan of most engaged couples to eventually buy a house. If this is true for you, then perhaps the best wedding present you could get would be a down payment on a home. Thanks to the unique program at this Uniondale, New York, bank, you can actually register for a mortgage.

A bank senior vice president came up with the concept after she'd learned a friend had received an expensive tea set and three espresso makers for her wedding, all of which she'd returned for cash. The idea behind this registry is simple: friends and family make cash contributions to a savings account that Bank America Mortgage has set up in your name. You don't have to get your mortgage through Bank America Mortgage, but if you do, the bank will waive the $100 closing fee.

This program is only available to residents in the following states: Arizona, Connecticut, Delaware, Maryland, Massachusetts, Michigan, New York, New Jersey, Pennsylvania, and Virginia.

For more information, call (800) 272-6791 Monday through Friday from 8:30 A.M. to 5:30 P.M. eastern time.

BARBECUE HALL OF FLAME
5015 Kirby   (713) 529-1212
Houston, TX 77098

👫

If you are a real meat-and-potatoes person, you're going to love Barbecue Hall of Flame. This

Houston shop lets you register for things that would make any redblooded, meat lover go crazy. You can request cuts of wild game meats—buffalo, elk, venison, and boar—and barbecue pits to cook them in.

These are not your ordinary backyard grills, mind you. The barbecue pits that Barbecue Hall of Flame sells run from 30 inches in length to about 48 inches and range in price from $595 to $1,395. They're true smokers because they smoke the meat instead of grilling it. Besides the pits, you can also register for cooking utensils, knives, barbecue sauces and rubs, and cookbooks so you'll know how to do the meat up just right.

You don't have to stick to a barbecue theme when registering here. The store also sells all types of Western clothing, including a line for guys that looks circa 1890s and another for gals called Cadillac Cowgirl, which looks very 1950s.

A salesperson at the store will read your out-of-town guests your wish list over the phone, take a credit card order, and arrange to have gifts delivered. Not surprisingly, gifts purchased from Barbecue Hall of Flame can't be gift wrapped, because either they're too big or they might leak.

Barbecue Hall of Flame is open Monday through Wednesday from 10:00 A.M. to 6:00 P.M., Thursday through Saturday from 10:00 A.M. to 9:00 P.M., and Sunday from 10:00 A.M. to 6:00 P.M. central time.

GOOD VIBRATIONS

1210 Valencia Street   (415) 974-8980
(flagship store)   (800) 289-8423
San Francisco, CA 94110

🚶 ☎

Don't be fooled into thinking this San Francisco

shop specializes in Beach Boys music. Good
Vibrations is a place where open-minded couples
with a healthy sexual appetite go for sexual toys,
books, and videos. Good Vibrations stocks literally thousands of items, ranging from massage oil
and feathers to leather restraints and high-
powered vibrators. The store also includes a
vibrator museum, in case you're interested.

There are two stores in the Bay Area—one in
San Francisco and one in Berkeley—and most
couples who register here live locally. There are
also two catalogs, allowing out-of-towners who
might be interested in registering here to see
what's available. One catalog has the same name as
the store and includes toys and such; the other,
Sexuality Library, is strictly books and tapes. Call
(800) 289-8423 to request the catalogs. Even
though you might use a catalog as your registry
guide, you'll still need to register your preferences
by calling one of the retail shops.

Your guests can visit one of the two shops to
access your list, or if they prefer to shop incog-
nito, they can make purchases over the phone.
Good Vibrations has a fairly liberal return policy,
but there are some things you cannot return, like
intimate apparel. Most returns will be accepted in
exchange for something else in the store.

You and your guests can call (800) 289-8423
Monday through Saturday from 7:00 A.M. to 7:00
P.M. Both Good Vibrations stores are open
Monday through Sunday from 11:00 A.M. to 7:00
P.M. pacific time.

I.C. LONDON

1419 East Boulevard   (704) 377-7955
Suite F
Charlotte, NC 28203

Women who register at lingerie shop I.C. London
do so "because they're looking for something
better than average, something different from
what they might find at mass-market retailers,"
says owner Shelly Gilbert. Her 1,000-square-foot
store in the historic Dilworth district of Charlotte
carries high-end designer lingerie (Christian Dior
and Eileen West, for example), sleepwear, and
loungewear plus accessories, such as slippers,
panty hose, and soaps. Most of the store's stock is
for women, but Gilbert does stock silk boxer
shorts and robes for men.

"If she's having a lingerie shower thrown for
her, (I can) put together a really nice trousseau for
her," adds Gilbert, who works one-on-one with all
customers who register here. She'll make note of
the bride's sizes, fabric, and color preferences, and
she'll encourage the bride to try items on so she'll
know ahead of time if they fit and look good on
her. Plus, this gives Gilbert a sense of what the
bride's personal style is. All of this information is
kept in Gilbert's handwritten registry book. She
may even add to the bride's wish list such specific
information as "she wears only gowns and does
not want to receive any pajamas."

Having detailed descriptions of the bride's
likes and dislikes makes working with guests much
easier, since many call from out of town and speak
with Gilbert over the phone. "They'll tell me what
their budget is, and I can make recommendations,"
she says. If a guest isn't comfortable purchasing

lingerie per se, Gilbert will recommend a gift certificate instead. She'll gift wrap any purchases for free and hold them at the store until the guests get to town for the wedding. Or if the shower is being thrown somewhere else, she'll ship the package via UPS.

I.C. London is open Monday through Saturday from 10:00 A.M. to 6:00 P.M. eastern time.

INTIMATE BOOKSHOP

Eastgate Shopping Center   (919) 929-0414
1800 East Franklin Street   (800) 835-3289
(flagship store)
Chapel Hill, NC 27514

Intimate Bookshop is a chain of 10 bookstores in North Carolina that stocks literally hundreds of thousands of book titles. The store's name harks back to 1931, the year it first opened, when it was a small, intimate bookstore near the University of North Carolina–Chapel Hill campus. Today, the store sells hardback and paperback fiction and nonfiction titles, ranging from *New York Times* bestsellers to cookbooks to medical reference books.

The idea for a registry came a couple of years ago from a Chapel Hill couple who were regular customers and decided that what they really wanted for wedding gifts were books. They came in, discussed the idea with the manager, and then created a wish list that was kept on file. "They picked out all sorts of books that they'd always admired but couldn't afford," recalls Shannon Wilke, a store employee. "They made a list and listed the price of each book beside the title, and then the manager distributed copies to all the stores."

The registry process is still informal at all 10 locations in Chapel Hill, Raleigh, Winston-Salem, Greensboro, Fayetteville, Charlotte, and Goldsboro. Just ask to speak with a manager and let him or her know that store number 5 in Chapel Hill has done a registry before, and you should have no problem picking out the books you'd like to receive and formulating a registry list. The manager at the store where you register should automatically send your list to all the other stores, but a gentle reminder to have this done might not hurt. Employees will use internal E-mail to keep each other updated on purchases so duplicates can be avoided.

If your guests live out of town, they can call Intimate Bookshop's toll-free number, (800) 835-3289, to order books and have them shipped. Or they can call the store where you registered. Folks who buy gifts in person have the option of having any book priced over $25 gift wrapped for free. Returns are for store credit only.

Intimate Bookshop store hours vary based on location.

LOVER'S LANE
2020 Wayne Road   (313) 728-5100
(flagship store)
Westland, MI 48185
👫

It isn't just lingerie-themed bridal showers that inspire brides to register at Lover's Lane—couples sometimes register for a bachelor or bachelorette party, too. Lover's Lane, with five stores in the Detroit area, is a combination lingerie store and sexual aid shop. In the past, the following have showed up on wish lists: Kamasutra products, such as massage creams and lotions, and edible dusting powders and balms; books on massage; and a white corselet with sequins and beads and matching garter belts. "Many brides go for erotica and exotic items," says Laurie Schwartz, manager of the Novi store.

It takes a couple of hours for a bride to register, especially if she's requesting lingerie, because she needs to try everything on. Since most guests shop at the store where the bride has registered, Lover's Lane won't automatically send a wish list to the other four stores, but that can be done, if requested.

Out-of-town guests may have a tough time shopping here, since the store won't take credit card orders over the phone. "We don't know who we're dealing with and we want to cut down on credit card fraud," says Schwartz. As long as they plan ahead, guests can mail a check for a purchase and then request that it be shipped.

Schwartz has noticed an interesting trend among guests who visit her store. "They want to buy what they want the bride to have, not what the bride wants. Most of the moms and grand-mothers ooh and aah over the long, pretty stuff," she says. But if the bride has requested only G-strings and push-up bras, "I'll encourage them to buy what the bride wants," she adds. If they won't listen, then Schwartz might suggest a gift certifi-cate instead. This way, everyone ends up happy.

Everything in the store can be gift wrapped for $1.50. Nothing can be returned "due to the personal nature of the garments," Schwartz explains.

All Lover's Lane locations are open Monday

through Saturday from 10:00 A.M. to 9:00 P.M. and Sunday from 12:00 noon to 6:00 P.M. eastern time. However, between Memorial Day and Labor Day, the stores are closed on Sunday.

LOWE'S HOME CENTERS ☛ *Home Improvement*

METROPOLITAN MUSEUM OF ART SHOPS ☛ *Home Decor*

PRAIRIE AVENUE BOOKSHOP
711 South Dearborn   (312) 922-8311
Chicago, IL 60605   (800) 474-2724
🚶 ✉

Being able to register at Prairie Avenue Bookshop is a dream come true for architects across the country. That's because this is an architectural specialty bookshop carrying thousands of works detailing the designs of architects around the world. The store also sells lithographs and plates that showcase architectural drawings by such greats as Frank Lloyd Wright and others. Book prices range from $50 to $150.

You can visit this downtown Chicago bookstore in person to register. Just submit your wish list to the manager. Or you can request a copy of the store's catalog over the phone by calling (800) 474-2724, check off the books you like, and mail the list back to the store. The most recent catalog has 96 pages of biographies of architects, glossy books of interiors, titles on technical drawings, and periodicals.

The store is used to taking mail-order requests from all over the world, so having your guests order gifts over the phone shouldn't be a problem. Returns are for store credit only.

You and your guests can call (800) 474-2724 during business hours, which are Monday through Friday from 9:30 A.M. to 5:30 P.M. and Saturday from 10:00 a.m to 4:00 P.M. central time.

REAL GOODS TRADING CORPORATION
555 Leslie Street   (800) 762-7325
Ukiah, CA 95482-5507

Some people joke that the Real Goods Trading Corporation is the Sears Roebuck of alternative energy. They're right in that like Sears, Real Goods tends to sell everything under the sun. And, speaking of the sun, many of these products, available through the Real Goods Trading Corporation catalog or at the three store locations in California, Oregon, and Wisconsin, are solar-powered. Items available range from the rechargeable lawn mower to a solar charging panel for your camcorder to a solar-powered flashlight.

Alternative-energy products are what generate the most registry business for Real Goods, but that isn't the only category of products from which you can choose. The second most popular merchandise for the soon-to-be-married is the company's line of environmentally friendly bedding. This line includes 200-thread-count sheets made from 100 percent unbleached combed cotton that is free of resins, dyes, and formaldehyde, making these sheets hypoallergenic. The store's pillows are popular too. They come in two varieties—wool- or cotton-filled. The cotton is guaranteed to be organically grown.

Real Goods Trading Corporation also carries kitchen accessories, such as coffee filters made from 23-karat gold and a recycled can compacter; tools for the garden and home, such as lamps in which you can use Real Goods Trading Corporation's energy-efficient bulbs, organic cleaning products, and handwoven rugs made from natural jute fiber and reclaimed cotton rags; plus books on every environmental topic imaginable (titles include *Wind Power for Home and Business* by Paul Gipe [Chelsea Green Publishing Company, 1995] and *Solar Living Sourcebook* by Real Goods Trading Corporation).

Even though the corporation has three retail locations, you must register with Cindy Boyman through the mail-order division at (800) 762-7325. She'll mail you a catalog and then work with you by phone or fax to put together your wish list. Then, she'll copy it and distribute it to the stores, giving your guests the option of buying gifts for you through the catalog or at one of the stores. The stores keep her posted via E-mail on any purchases made so you won't get two or three of the same items. Any returns must be handled through the customer service department, accessible through the toll-free number.

"Most of our clientele is between 25 and 35 years old," says Boyman, "and they're very environmentally conscious in all aspects of their lives."

You and your guests can call the Real Goods Trading Corporation bridal registry hotline, (800) 762-7325, Monday through Friday from 6:00 A.M. to 8:00 P.M. and Saturday from 8:00 A.M. to 6:00 P.M. pacific time. Business hours at the three retail stores vary by location.

THE SEVENTH GENERATION CATALOG

☛ *Bath and Bedding*

SHERRY-LEHMANN
679 Madison Avenue
New York, NY 10021
🚶 ✉ ☎

(212) 838-7500

Registering at this wine seller on New York City's chic Upper East Side is perfect for the couple who considers themselves wine connoisseurs. The selection, however, can be overwhelming—there are more than 5,000 wines to choose from. Therefore, it's best to set aside a couple of hours for traipsing up and down the store's aisles or make sure you know exactly what you want before you arrive.

Store owner Michael Aaron says he gets only about 30 registry requests each year, so you're sure to get excellent service should you decide to register here. According to Aaron, one of the bestsellers on the bridal registry continues to be the 1990 wines, which he describes as a great vintage year. "We usually find people will register for a Bordeaux and then some younger vintages that they can lay down," he says. "However, people have registered for their favorite cognac as well."

Aaron will gladly accept a registry list over the phone from a couple out of state and then ship guests' purchases to them. However, only the following states and district allow alcohol to be shipped across state lines: California, District of Columbia, Florida, Idaho, Illinois, Michigan, New Jersey, New Mexico, New York, Oregon, Washington, and Wisconsin.

Store hours are Monday through Saturday from 10:00 A.M. to 7:00 P.M. eastern time.

TOWER RECORDS

22 East 4th Street   (800) 648-4844
(flagship store)   FAX: (800) 538-6938
New York, NY 10003

Even though Tower Records has approximately 70 stores nationwide, registering must be done through the company's mail-order division in New York. However, you might want to visit one of the stores before compiling your list, as Tower's selection is extensive.

Registry selections here have really run the gamut. Some couples have registered for the complete works of the Beatles and Beethoven, others for The Lemonheads, R.E.M., and Garth Brooks. Besides compact discs and tapes, you can also register for movies on videotape and laser disc.

Once you've compiled your list, mail or fax it and your wedding guest list to Tower's toll-free number, (800) 538-6938. Tower Records likes to have both lists at least two weeks before gift giving might commence so it can be sure to have items in stock and ready to ship. Plus, by having the guest list on hand, the store can keep track of who's bought what. You must also include a cutoff date after which your guests will no longer be able to make purchases. This window of time allows for all deliveries to arrive—they are usually sent by UPS standard delivery, which can take up to two weeks. Your registry will be active as soon as Tower Records receives both lists.

If for any reason you change your mind after the wedding and want to return items from your registry, you can return the items at a Tower Records location or do everything through the mail-order division. Tower Records will gladly credit your charge card or give you a store credit.

Operators are available at (800) 648-4844 Monday through Friday from 8:00 A.M. to 10:00 P.M. and Saturday and Sunday from 10:00 A.M. to 7:00 P.M. eastern time.

TREVA'S

7200 West Alameda Avenue (303) 922-3671
Denver, CO 80226

Silk seems to be the fabric of choice for brides who register at Treva's, a Denver lingerie store. Most women who are registering for a lingerie shower seem to go for tap pants and a camisole or a teddy with a short robe, but two-piece ensembles aren't all you can choose from here. The store also sells gloves, garters, bras, and Kama-sutra products, such as oils and massage creams. Guys also get into the idea of registering for lingerie by choosing from silk robes, G-strings, and boxer shorts.

It's best to register at Treva's in person about two months prior to your shower or wedding. You'll be given a sheet of paper and then free reign of the store so you can try items on and write down a description of your choices including the colors you prefer and the size you take. Your wish list will be kept on file for a few months after your wedding.

Guests who shop in person will be given one-on-one service so they'll have an easy time finding merchandise from your registry. Those who prefer to shop over the phone might be encouraged to go with a gift certificate. "It's kind of hard to pick something for someone else, especially without seeing it," explains Phyllis, a store salesperson. Anything over $75 will be gift wrapped for free. And as long as a purchased item has not been worn or soiled or isn't crotchless to begin with, it can be exchanged.

Treva's is open Monday through Friday from 10:00 A.M. to 9:00 P.M., Saturday from 10:00 A.M. to 7:00 P.M., and Sunday from 11:00 a.m to 5:00 P.M. mountain time.

WINES OF AMERICA
2055 Westheimer   (713) 524-3397
Suite 155
(flagship store)
Houston, TX 77098

Most of the people who register at one of the two Wines of America locations in Houston have waited a little longer in life to get married or are registering for a subsequent marriage. All, however, are bona fide wine lovers. "We figure if they're combining wine racks when they tie the knot, our store is the perfect place for them to register," says Dean Michaels, manager of the Woodway store, who conceived the registry program in 1992.

You don't need an appointment to register here—you can just walk in off the street if you happen to be in the area. The only time that *isn't* good for registering is Friday evenings between 5:00 and 7:00, when the store holds its weekly wine tastings. However, if you're unsure of the kinds of wines you'd like to add to your wish list, a Friday evening wine tasting would be an excellent opportunity to sample the various vintages the store has to offer.

When you do register, you'll be given a form to fill out, which breaks out wines into categories, like chardonnay, merlot, and sparkling wines. If you need help making selections, a member of the store's knowledgeable sales staff will walk you through the store and quiz you on your wine likes and dislikes. "Then we can tailor their selections based on their responses," adds Michaels.

Since Wines of America stocks a huge selection of California wines as well as those from other wine producing regions in the United States, don't feel pressured to pick wines from every aisle; most registrants here pick just a few of their favorites. When guests come in to make purchases, a salesperson will help them obtain your registry list, walk them around the store, and make sure that you receive a well-rounded sampling of the wines on your wish list.

Because Wines of America won't ship across state lines or to certain areas in Texas (which are still "dry"), it's best to register here only if your guests are within driving distance of Houston. An added bonus for your guests who visit the store: the store provides a special paint pen that they can use to sign and write a special message on the bottle or bottles of wine they buy. This way, when you drink that special vintage, you'll always remember who bought it for you.

Store hours vary by location.

The Whole Kitchen Kaboodle

You've heard the saying that home is where the heart is. For some culinary types, it's also where the hearth is. By choosing to register at a store that focuses on kitchen accessories, you're more likely to get a line of cooking equipment that is of higher quality than that of a run-of-the-mill store. Many cooking-oriented stores also offer hands-on demonstrations that will help you see how your potential gifts selections will stand up in the kitchen.

These stores are also excellent places to register for everyday dishes and can offer a wider range of styles and colors than you might find elsewhere. Some of the stores have more than one location, guaranteeing your guests a larger stocked inventory from which to purchase your gifts.

ABC CARPET AND HOME	☛ *Bath and Bedding*
ACE HARDWARE	☛ *Home Improvement*
AL'S POTTERY, CHINA & SILVER	☛ *Fine China and Crystal*
BED, BATH & BEYOND	☛ *Bath and Bedding*
BERING'S	☛ *Fine China and Crystal*

BLACKHAWK HARDWARE
Park & Woodlawn Roads   (704) 525-2682
Park Road Shopping Center
Charlotte, NC 28209
🏃

Jim Wilkerson, owner of Blackhawk Hardware, never considered offering a registry service until a few years ago, when he noticed that a lot of people were coming to his store with department store registry lists in hand to buy merchandise. What attracted them to Blackhawk Hardware was not only the store's prices but its selection of housewares. "Most people like to buy in the $20 to $25 range, and we've got tons of stuff in that range," he says. "These items are fairly substantial and probably more practical in a lot of ways than, say, a $100 silver salt and pepper shaker set."

Couples who register at Blackhawk Hardware most often ask for canister sets, placemats, tea kettles, and pot racks, but asking for hoes and garbage cans isn't unheard of either. Many of the guys add tools to the list, too. Putting together a wish list is always done in person, and each couple gets a clipboard and preprinted form on which they can write their preferences. That form is then kept in a file cabinet until guests come in to buy gifts. "We've had people come from out of town at the last-minute and shop on Saturday morning for a Saturday evening wedding," adds Wilkerson. Lucky for these last-minute shoppers, Blackhawk offers a gift wrapping service; for any item under $50, it costs $2.50. Items costing more will be wrapped for free.

Guests who plan ahead can call the store, work with a salesperson over the phone to purchase a gift, and have the gift shipped via UPS to their or the engaged couple's home. The store records all purchases on a computer, so returns are a snap. Returns yield cash back or store credit.

Blackhawk Hardware is open Monday through Friday from 8:00 A.M. to 9:00 P.M., Saturday from 8:00 A.M. to 6:00 P.M., and Sunday from 1:00 P.M. to 6:00 P.M. eastern time.

C'EST LA VIE
24 Atlantic Avenue   (617) 639-2468
Marblehead, MA 01945
🚶🚶

With a selection of handmade pottery, California handblown glasses, French table linens, and small table accessories, C'est La Vie is the perfect place to register if you and your future spouse have an eclectic taste in kitchenware and small home furnishings. And because the store isn't very big—it's only 650 square feet—owner Cassandra Hughes likes to take the time to get to know all the brides and grooms who come into the store to register.

According to Hughes, who logs all wish lists in a special registry book, some of the most common pieces to turn up on registries are those made by Rhode Island potter Lark Rodriques. "All her pieces are handformed and handpainted with flowers on it," she says, "and because she was a gardener in Newport, all of her themes come from her working knowledge of the earth." Rodriques makes functional pieces, such as serving platters, bowls, plates, and trays, all of earthenware, many with sentimental thoughts painted on them, such as Home Sweet Home and May You Be Happy.

Couples who register at C'est La Vie, located in a seaside town on the north shore of Boston, also seem to be fond of Annie Glass platters and Union Glass goblets, which feature 24-karat gold leaf under the bowl and a very tall stem. "They mix well with traditional china," adds Hughes.

Because the inventory at C'est La Vie is always changing, Hughes recommends that all couples who register months in advance of their shower or wedding stop back occasionally to check out new merchandise. She also suggests that those who register for pieces that may be one of a kind choose second and third choices, just in case. However, Hughes will do whatever she can so that selected items are still around when guests visit the store or call on the phone to buy gifts. "If it's their glasses or serving pieces that they really want and there's a chance they'll be gone before guests come in, we'll set them aside," she says. "Some things are here today and gone tomorrow."

If selected items are gone and guests attempt to use their better judgment—and fail—by buying you something else, Hughes will gladly take anything back in exchange for another item in the store.

C'est La Vie is open Monday through Saturday from 10:00 A.M. to 5:00 P.M. and Sunday from 12:00 noon to 5:00 P.M. eastern time.

CHINA OUTLET AND GOURMET GARAGE

☛ *Fine China and Crystal*

CITY AND COUNTRY
50 Daniel Street
(flagship store)
Portsmouth, NH 03801
🏃

(603) 433-5353

The name of this store refers to its mix of home furnishings. Within the city realm are contemporary pieces like you'd expect to find in a well-to-do metropolitan home. The country aspect is more French countryside, featuring wrought iron garden furniture and blue-and-white-checked dinnerware. In between, however, is a dazzling range of home furnishings and cookware.

In fact, it is the cookware, kitchen, and dining accessories that attract most couples to City and Country, which has shops in Portsmouth, New Hampshire; Cresskill, New Jersey; Newburyport, Massachusetts; and Key West, Florida. Here, you'll find All-Clad, Calphalon, Chantal, and Cuisinart pots and pans, plus table linens, wooden spoons, and chef's carts. There's also glassware from Germany, Italy, France, and America and flatware too.

Other categories that seem to please registering couples are domestics, closet organizers, lifestyle (furnishing pieces like bookcases and end tables), home office, and seasonal items. "In the spring, garden furniture is really big, and a June bride can register for barbecue equipment if she likes," says Glen Gerace, a buyer for City and Country, "whereas a December bride might register for Christmas ornaments." Gerace says that guests enjoy giving Christmas ornaments "because it's like starting a tradition." The fact that they're affordable probably doesn't hurt either. Many of the couples who register here also say that they'll be happy to receive gift certificates as well.

Gerace doesn't encourage couples to register too many months before the wedding. "We warn people who register far in advance that their items may not be in the store by the next year," he says. "If they do, we encourage them to check back, look and see if there's anything new they want, and make additions to their registry." He adds that things like cookware and dinnerware don't readily go out of stock, so couples who are registering only for those items needn't worry.

When you register in person at one of the four stores, you'll be asked to jot down vendor codes and brief descriptions of the items you'd like. That information is then entered into the store's computer system within one to two working days. But be warned: even though the information is technically on-line, it doesn't always get to the other three stores. "If you have guests going to the other stores," Gerace suggests, "it would be best to specifically request that the information be sent to those stores at the get go."

Gerace often works with out-of-town guests who access a registry list, make purchases over the phone, and then request that the gift be held at the store until they come to town for the wedding. However, City and Country will ship to locations in the United States upon request as well.

Store hours vary by location.

COMPLEAT GOURMET AND GIFTS

7592 South University Boulevard   (303) 290-9222
Littleton, CO 80122   (800) 366-9222

Compleat Gourmet and Gifts is a kitchenware and housewares store that attracts couples who are getting away from traditional items and registering for things they can entertain with. They offer everything from small kitchen appliances to hand-made pottery to kitchen gadgets as well as cook-books and cooking gadgets.

Compleat Gourmet and Gifts is actually the sister store to Compleat Selection (See Fine China and Crystal), so couples often register in both stores, using Compleat Gourmet and Gifts to take care of all their kitchen needs. Registering in person takes about two to three hours, and many couples who register in both stores break the process into two days. When couples register here, a store bridal consultant will walk you through the process step by step and won't even let you pick up a pencil to write your preferences down—he or she will do it for you.

The registry is handwritten, and a copy of

your list is given to guests who visit the store in person. Or it can be mailed to those who prefer to shop by phone via the Compleat Gourmet and Gifts's toll-free number, (800) 366-9222. It's not uncommon for a store employee to handwrite a cover letter to these guests and make sure to include the prices of all the items on your wish list. Once a year, the store prints a catalog of merchandise, so if you register during October, November, or December, when the catalog is available, you can request that copies be sent to your guests. All gift purchases are wrapped for free.

You and your guests can call (800) 366-9222 during business hours, which are Monday through Friday from 9:30 A.M. to 6:00 P.M., Saturday from 9:30 A.M. to 5:30 P.M., and Sunday from 12:00 noon to 5:00 P.M. mountain time.

THE CONTAINER STORE   ☞ *Home Improvement*

A COOK'S WARES

211 37th Street   (412) 846-9490
Beaver Falls, PA 15010   FAX: (412) 846-9562

A Cook's Wares is the sort of catalog that will make any gourmet cook salivate. It has 64 pages of high-quality cookware, some of it at 20 to 40 percent off retail prices. The prices more than make up for the catalog's dull appearance. It is printed on newsprint and includes only line drawings of merchandise and no photographs.

Catalog categories include ingredients and condiments, like cooking sherry, Dean & Deluca honey mustard, and chocolate chips; pans, by such makers as All-Clad and Le Creuset; cookbooks, ranging from *Ice Cream! The Whole Scoop* by Gail Daneron (Glenbridge Publishing Ltd., 1995) to *Focaccia: Simple Breads from the Italian Oven* by Carol Field (Chronicle Books, 1995); porcelain dishes, for cooking casseroles and quiche; and pepper mills. The catalog comes out twice a year and always features specials. Recent ones included a sale on Krups blenders, knife sharpeners, and Cuisinart everyday pans.

A Cook's Wares also has a storefront at its headquarters, located 30 minutes outside Pittsburgh, so you can register in person as well. Most people, however, register through the catalog. All you need to do is write down the items you like, fax or mail the list back to A Cook's Wares, and then the company will send a copy of your list and a catalog to anyone you'd like.

Most items in the catalog are in stock, so A Cook's Wares promises that it will get most orders out within three days. The company ships via UPS. Your guests can request that a gift be wrapped, but it will cost them about $3 extra.

A Cook's Wares is open for business Monday through Friday from 9:00 A.M. to 4:00 P.M. and Saturday from 9:00 A.M. to 1:00 P.M. eastern time.

COOKWORKS

322 South Guadalupe Street	(505) 988-7676
Santa Fe, NM 87501	(800) 972-3357

Because Cookworks is actually three stores in one—Cookworks Tabletop, Cookworks Gourmet Foods, and Cookworks Cookware—it works best for people to register separately in the tabletop store and then do a combined registry in the gourmet and equipment stores.

Cookworks Tabletop specializes in nontraditional dinnerware, including great lines of Italian and domestic dinnerware and flatware. You won't find anything like bone china in this store. Instead, you'll find dishes and serving pieces that have been handpainted, like the line of dishes by a local potter who gives a real Southwestern flare to his work—everything is made from Santa Fe clay and is very colorful. You might think of the wares in this store as "casual elegant." Included along with dishes are one-of-a-kind, antique French silverware, including flatware and serving pieces, plus a variety of porcelain made by potters all over the world. Cookworks Tabletop also stocks table linens, handblown glasses, and even though it may seem a bit askew from the store's kitchen theme, European soaps and beauty products.

Cookworks Gourmet Foods smells great because it's a shop that carries a full line of gourmet coffees, teas, and chocolate. You'll also find a wide variety of food items, such as Italian pastas and other sorts of regional fare. Believe it or not, these perishables can be added to your wish list as well.

In Cookworks Cookware you'll find the store's wide selection of cooking equipment. Makers on display include Le Creuset, Calphalon, Cuisinart, Chantal, Borjeag (a line of copper pots and pans), All-Clad, and KitchenAid. Besides pots and pans, this shop has cookbooks, antique stoves, bread machines, blenders, whisks, wooden spoons, mixing bowls, bakeware, dish towels, and German knives.

When you register at Cookworks, one of the salespeople will walk you through the three stores and help educate you on what's available. They will spend a lot of time pulling things together, coordinating linens and dishes and helping you to put together a beautiful table.

Cookworks does a tremendous amount of business with guests who are buying gifts from afar. This is one of the reasons the shop offers a toll-free number: (800) 972-3357. When out-of-towners call, a salesperson will spend as much time as he or she needs with them on the phone, attempting to describe the items you've chosen and give them a picture of what your finished table looks like. Then, the store will wrap any purchases for free and ship them.

Your guests can call (800) 972-3357 during Cookworks business hours, Monday through Friday from 10:00 A.M. to 5:30 P.M., Saturday 9:30 A.M. to 5:30 P.M., and Sunday, 11:00 A.M. to 5:00 P.M. mountain time.

COTTONWOOD CUPBOARD ☛ *Fine China and Crystal*

CRATE & BARREL
725 Landwehr Road   (800) 967-6696
(corporate headquarters)
Northbrook, IL 60062-2393

For couples looking for lighthearted, classic, and affordable housewares, Crate & Barrel is a great place to register. In fact, many of today's brides and grooms who decide to register at more than one store most likely end up choosing Crate & Barrel because of its selection of dinnerware, cooking equipment and utensils, bath and bedding accessories, and furniture. This is the kind of store where you can find anything, and prices range from $1.95 to $195.00 and more.

Another bonus to registering at Crate & Barrel: you don't need to live near one of its 51 stores to register here. There are Crate & Barrel stores in only 12 states plus Washington, D.C., and the store understands that there are engaged couples living elsewhere who would like to register with the company. To meet their needs, Crate & Barrel offers a long-distance bridal registry kit, which you can request by calling the store's gift registry hotline, (800) 967-6696.

In this kit you'll find six brochures. One gives an overview of Crate & Barrel's registry (all registry choices are entered into the nationwide computer registry 72 hours after your wish list is received, the registry is updated every 24 hours to avoid duplicates, and so forth). The remaining five brochures are each devoted to different categories of Crate & Barrel merchandise: dinnerware, flat-ware, stemware, barware, and cookware. Each registry kit also comes with a price list and a wish-list form to fill out. Once it's completed, you can return it to Crate & Barrel in the enclosed postage-paid envelope.

The dinnerware brochure, for example, lets you know that you can choose from three different kinds of dishes—porcelain, earthenware, and stoneware—and explains how the three differ. A gatefold in the brochure opens up to show color pictures of 24 different patterns available, ranging from a simple ivory basketweave design to the colorful, handpainted "Martinique," which is reminiscent of Gaugin's paintings of the South Pacific.

Just because the registry kit talks only about certain kitchen items doesn't mean that you're limited to these five categories when completing your wish list. On the contrary, the entire contents of the Crate & Barrel stores (if you live near one) and catalog (which you can request be sent to you) can be included as well. One couple who'd just purchased a house registered for a hammock and four Adirondack chairs. Other unusual items that often make it onto registries include anything having to do with coffee (espresso makers and oversized latte cups and saucers), ethnic cooking (pasta makers, woks, and fondue pots) and country-inspired furniture (Italian bistro chairs and pine tables).

For some time now, wedding guests nationwide have perked up considerably when they learned that the engaged couple has registered at Crate & Barrel. That's because the store's registry system is extremely easy for them to use. They just pop by a store and request a copy of the list at the customer service desk or call the 800 number and request that one be sent to them. The registry list itself is extremely easy to read and includes the prices of items. That way, if your guests have a price range in mind, they can use the list as a guide. Your guests also have these options: buying a gift at a store, ordering something through the catalog, or calling the store where you registered and making a purchase directly from that location.

Crate & Barrel will keep your registry information on file for six months after your wedding. If you have any returns to make, you can bring them to any store location.

Operators are available at the gift registry hotline, (800) 967-6696, Monday through Friday from 9:00 A.M. to 5:00 P.M. central time. Store hours vary by location.

DANSK

108 Corporate Park Drive   (800) 293-2675
(corporate headquarters)
White Plains, NY 10604

🚶 📖

Dansk is a great place to register if you and your fiancé haven't quite decided on a look for your kitchen and want the option of mixing and matching your dinnerware, flatware, and glassware. Unlike many manufacturers, which sell patterns in five-piece place settings, most Dansk patterns are available with three or four pieces per setting. This allows you to mix and match pieces from other settings.

Most Dansk pieces are made from porcelain, although there are some stoneware designs, such as "Mesa," which looks like it was plucked right from the desert southwest, and others are hand-painted ceramics. Dansk flatware is as versatile as the dinnerware, and you can choose from stainless steel or silver plate in 16 different designs. Stemware runs the gamut, from the bulbous "Hanna" to the very geometric "Karin." Versatility is the norm with Dansk table linens and serving pieces, too.

Dansk has approximately 60 retail locations in 28 states. Five of these stores are considered lifestyle stores and stock larger quantities of first-run merchandise. These lifestyle stores are located in Beverly Hills; La Jolla, California; Denver; Portland, Oregon; and Bellevue, Washington. The remaining locations are outlet stores, which often carry seconds, discontinued merchandise, special purchases, and test pieces. You can pick up a bridal registry packet containing a catalog, registry form, and list of stores nationwide at any store, and you can register at any location. If you choose to register at one of outlet stores, you will be forewarned that you might be requesting items that have been discontinued and therefore might not be replaceable.

Registries at Dansk are not kept on-line, and wish lists are not sent from one store to all the others. You can request that your list be sent to other store locations if you have guests who live in the area, but that's not commonly done here. Instead, your guests will probably have to work primarily with the store where you registered. "They can do mail order, but it has to be arranged with each individual store," says Lisa Larsen, a Dansk consumer relations supervisor. If a gift is shipped, it won't be gift wrapped—the stores don't offer that service—but a gift card will be enclosed.

Even though your guests may not be able to access your registry and shop at any Dansk location, you can make returns at any of them. You'll be issued a store credit or allowed to exchange one item for another.

To find a Dansk store nearest you, call Dansk headquarters at (800) 293-2675. Store hours vary by location.

EDDIE BAUER HOME COLLECTION
14850 N.E. 36th Street   (800) 645-7467
(corporate headquarters)
Redmond, WA 98052
🚶

When you used to walk by an Eddie Bauer Home Collection store, you'd see rustic-looking log beds, denim-covered couches, and lots of accessories with moose and geese on them. That is no longer true. While the stores still hold on to the original outdoorsy Eddie Bauer theme—for example, the denim-covered couch still prevails—more and more of the merchandise the stores carry is classic and contemporary. Not surprisingly, more couples are attracted to the stores' new and improved look and are registering here.

Even though Eddie Bauer Home Collection stores carry furniture and small home furnishings, such as frames and candles, most of the couples who register here do so for the dinnerware, flatware, stemware, table linens, and bath and bedding products.

Most of the plates, glasses, forks, knives, and spoons that Eddie Bauer carries are Eddie Bauer exclusives, including two dinnerware designs that are made specially for Eddie Bauer by Pfaltzgraff. One Pfaltzgraff design, "Leaf Garland," is sage green stoneware that features an ivory ivy leaf pattern. Other dining accessories are just as earthy. Take, for example, the "Aspen" flatware. With its wooden handles, it is simultaneously outdoorsy and timeless. In addition, most of the glassware at the Eddie Bauer Home Collection works equally well outdoors by the pool as it does inside on a well-dressed dining room table.

The store's Egyptian cotton towels seem to attract a lot of attention from the registering crowd—probably because they are made from a high-grade, superabsorbent cotton, are cut larger than the average bath towel, and come in 12 different colors ranging from salmon to amethyst to gray flannel. The down comforters and pillows are popular, too. And why not? With a respective thread count of 200 and 270, this kind of bedding is extraordinarily soft to the touch.

It's too bad you can't register through the Eddie Bauer Home Collection catalog; the registry files at the stores have nothing to do with the mail-order division. In addition, unless you specifically request it, the store where you register won't send your list to the other 18 or so Eddie Bauer Home Collection stores. But if you do ask for this to be done, the store manager at the location where you registered will do his or her best to make sure that the information gets dispersed properly and that the master list gets updated.

Your friends and family can visit or call an Eddie Bauer Home Collection store that has your registry on file and work with a salesperson over the phone. The store will box any purchase—but will not gift wrap it—and ship it. To find the store nearest them, guests can call Eddie Bauer's store locator number, (800) 645-7467. If they want a copy of the catalog so they're not shopping blindly, they'll have to call the mail-order department, at (800) 426-8020, and request one. That's because the stores receive only a limited amount of catalogs and don't readily mail them to customers.

The toll-free, store locator telephone number, (800) 645-7467, is available 24 hours a day. Eddie Bauer Home Collection store hours vary by location.

FELISSIMO ☛ *Home Decor*

FROST & BUDD LTD. ☛ *Home Improvement*

GEARY'S ☛ *Fine China and Crystal*

GIFT N GOURMET

55 Old Santa Fe Trail   (505) 982-5953
Santa Fe, NM 87501

The real reason you'd want to register in this chaotic little store on the Plaza in Santa Fe is that it has a unique collection of tableware. One of the most popular brands in the store is Mamaro, a stoneware that's made in Italy and is painted bright red. Dishes and serving pieces from Mamaro really make a table interesting to look at. Because this is Santa Fe and the desert southwest, dinnerware with anything Native American on it is popular as well. One locally made stoneware collection, painted in a stark black and white, features *cocapelis*, profiles of Native American dancers, often playing the flute.

At Gift n Gourmet, you'll also find handblown goblets with bears or *cocapelis* on them and serving pieces such as taco holders and bean pots. A bean pot is a really neat contraption that looks almost like a punch bowl, but instead of glasses hanging from the loops on the bowl's outer lip, there are small bowls in which you can serve individual portions of beans.

Registering here is fairly simple—once you get past the crowds that often converge on the store. Just get a piece of paper from the manager and write down what you like; that information is kept on file. Guests who want to shop by phone can have the list read to them, use a credit card to pay for the purchase, and have it shipped. Gift wrapping is free.

Gift n Gourmet is open Monday through Saturday from 9:00 A.M. to 5:30 P.M. and Sunday from 9:00 a.m to 5:00 P.M. mountain time.

GUMP'S	☛ *Fine China and Crystal*
THE HAY LOFT SHOPS	☛ *Fine China and Crystal*
HOMEPLACE	☛ *Bath and Bedding*
KITCHEN ETC.	☛ *Fine China and Crystal*

KITCHEN KAPERS
301 Cherry Hill Mall   (609) 662-1919
(flagship store)
Cherry Hill, NJ 08002

Coffee is big business at Kitchen Kapers, a chain of 11 stores in Delaware, New Jersey, and Pennsylvania. Right now, tons of brides and grooms are registering for French press coffee makers, cappuccino makers, and coffee by the pound. Two of the most popular manufacturers of coffee appliances featured at Kitchen Kapers are Braun and Krups. At two of the New Jersey stores, you can even buy coffee by the cup and sip it while you're registering.

The sales staff at Kitchen Kapers won't let you register for any old item just because it seems nice. A sales associate will walk you around the store, talk to you about your decorating and entertaining style, and then compare and contrast various makers of small electronics (such as Cuisinart and KitchenAid), dishes, and cookware gadgets so you can be sure that you're getting something that best serves your needs. And, for example, if you haven't quite got the hang of steaming milk but really want a cappuccino maker, a salesperson will show you how to do it before marking the item down on your wish list. This kind of hands-on knowledge by the sales staff about the store's merchandise really sets Kitchen Kapers apart from other stores in the area.

Kitchen Kapers also stocks everyday dishes and a limited line of fine china. Portmeirion, for example, is its bestseller. It has Nambe serving pieces as well. And because the store's buyers go abroad every year to see what's new and hot in glassware and dishes, you can also find an ever-changing selection of European-made kitchen-ware. This year, the hot new item is tricolored glassware from Italy.

If you think your guests will be shopping at a Kitchen Kapers location other than the one where you registered, you'll need to specifically request that your wish list be sent to the other stores.

Because Kitchen Kapers has 11 locations, odds are your guests will never be faced with a back order on an item. That's because when inventory is running low at one store, a salesperson can call one of the other locations and get merchandise from there.

During the holiday season, Kitchen Kapers publishes a catalog, which your guests can use when shopping for you. The rest of the year, they can visit a store or speak with a sales associate over the phone. Kitchen Kapers will take a credit card order, gift wrap the item for free, and either hold the merchandise at the store until the shower or wedding or ship it via UPS.

Kitchen Kapers store hours vary by location.

KITCHEN PORT

415 North Fifth Avenue (313) 665-9188
(flagship store)   (800) 832-7678
Ann Arbor, MI 48104   FAX: (313) 665-8052

If you are a couple of cooking fanatics who are dying to add to your collection of Calphalon cookware, then you've got to register here. That's because Kitchen Port is the national dealer for Calphalon, based in nearby Toledo, Ohio. Because of this, you're going to find a larger selection of Calphalon products at this store than anywhere else in the country.

It's sad but true that the guests of couples who register for Calphalon at local department stores often end up at Kitchen Port because of the selection and great prices. "We always call the department store and let them know that something has been purchased," admits a Kitchen Port salesperson.

Because of its Calphalon connection, Kitchen Port is used to registering brides from all over the country. If you don't live in Ann Arbor, you can call your wish list in to the store's toll-free number, (800) 832-7678 or fax it to (313) 665-8052. Otherwise, you'll need to visit the store's Kerrytown location to register in person. (There is a second store in Ann Arbor, but the selection there isn't as great as at the Kerrytown store.) Just pick up a registry form and write down the ID number of the merchandise you'd like to receive. Your information will be kept on file for a year. After your registry is complete, you'll receive a cutting board as a thank-you gift. Note: don't try to register on Wednesday or Saturday when Ann Arbor's popular farmer's market is open. Kitchen

Port is located adjacent to the market, and on these two days, the store is extremely busy.

Your guests can shop at either Kitchen Port location because your wish list is available at both. Or they can call the toll-free number, which connects them to the Kerrytown store, and order off the registry. Their purchase will be wrapped and delivered for free as long as they spend over $25. During the holiday season, Kitchen Port puts out a catalog, which it will send to guests upon request.

Besides Calphalon cookware, Kitchen Port also carries cast-iron enameled cookware by Le Creuset of France. The store's collection of glassware is great, most notably the everyday and somewhat formal wine glasses and barware by German maker Schott. In addition, you'll find table linens, pepper mills, and KitchenAid food processors and mixers on Kitchen Port's shelves.

You and your guests can call (800) 832-7678 during Kitchen Port's business hours, which are Monday through Friday from 9:30 A.M. to 8:00 P.M., Saturday from 9:00 A.M. to 6:00 P.M., and Sunday from 11:00 A.M. to 5:00 P.M. eastern time.

LANAC SALES ☞ *Fine China and Crystal*

LANDS' END ☞ *Bath and Bedding*

LAURA ASHLEY ☞ *Bath and Bedding*

LEAF & BEAN
83 Seventh Avenue   (718) 638-5791
Brooklyn, NY 11217

Twenty years ago, Leaf & Bean was a small store-front that served gourmet tea and coffee (thus the name) to those living in Park Slope, a residential Brooklyn neighborhood. Over time, the store evolved into a specialty food store and then into one selling small electrical appliances and mugs that complemented its expanding line of coffee and tea.

Today, Leaf & Bean is a full-scale housewares store. Here your registry can really run the gamut. You can register for items true to Leaf & Bean's roots—coffee, tea, and food—as well as Krups coffeemakers and stainless steel flatware. You can also request porcelain and glassware from German manufacturers Lindt-Stymeist and Schott, respectively. In addition, the store stocks a large selection of handthrown earthenware imported from Italy and Portugal, all of which is FDA-approved to be lead free and nontoxic.

Leaf & Bean has a registry form that you fill out in person, and when your guests buy things, it is updated. Anything that is bought in the store will be gift wrapped for free and, if your guests choose, shipped to your home address. Returns are accepted at any time for an even exchange as long as the gift item wasn't on sale when it was purchased or isn't a seasonal item that the store no longer stocks.

Leaf & Bean is open Monday through Wednesday, 8:00 A.M. to 8:00 P.M., Thursday and Friday from 8:00 A.M. to 9:00 P.M., and Saturday

and Sunday from 9:00 A.M. to 7:00 P.M. eastern
time.

L.L. BEAN ☞ *Sporting Goods*

METROPOLITAN ☞ *Home Decor*
MUSEUM OF ART SHOPS

MICHAEL C. FINA ☞ *Fine China and*
  Crystal

OFF THE WALL
616 Canyon Road   (505) 983-8337
Santa Fe, NM 87501   (505) 982-5914
🚶 ☎

Off the Wall has the coolest collection of teapots,
stocking as many as 120 different kinds at a time.
They range from a bronze design that looks like
something a colonial house might have had in its
kitchen to one that is shaped like a monkey who
seems to be doing a jig. The teapots, like all the
other objets d'art that Off the Wall stocks, are
functional—you can actually fill these teapots with
water, put them on a stove top, and make yourself
a spot of tea. However, most of the people who
buy these gorgeous pieces, priced from $50 to
$500, keep them on display on a shelf rather than
using them.

Most of the brides and grooms who've registered here have been on vacation in Santa Fe and
have so fallen in love with the whimsical pieces
this shop–art gallery stocks that they just had to
register here. If you too are smitten, owner
Therese Bischeglia (a handmade paper and clay
artist in her own right) will sit down with you and
talk with you about what your needs are. "For

example, I'll find out if you want dinnerware or just accent pieces," says Bischeglia. She'll write down your selected pieces on an index card and then work with your guests over the phone. Most of the time, Bischeglia will send family and friends photographs of items in the store so they can see the sorts of things you've registered for. "Then, if they like the photographs, we'll take a credit card order and ship the item to them," she adds.

Besides teapots, Off the Wall carries seven different kinds of flatware, all of which look nothing like what you'd find in a department store. One flatware designer, Michael Aram, makes bronze and silver-plated pieces that are very wavy. Alone Larsen, another flatware maker, works with sandblasted stainless steel.

Off the Wall's dinnerware is as unique as the teapots and flatware. One potter, Robin Spear, creates earthenware painted in black and white. But instead of leaving the plates, bowls, and cups plain, she carves stars and moons into the clay and then paints them purple, turquoise, or red, giving the pieces a nice accent.

If you don't have the chance to get to Santa Fe but it sounds like Off the Wall stocks the kinds of unique things you and your spouse-to-be would like to receive as wedding gifts, give Bischeglia a call. She'll be glad to send you pictures of pieces in the store and work with you over the phone in putting together your ideal wish list.

Between April 15th and September 1st, Off the Wall is open daily from 10:00 A.M. to 6:00 P.M.; at other times during the year, it's open 9:00 A.M. to 5:00 P.M. mountain time.

PACIFIC LINEN	☛ *Bath and Bedding*
PRATESI LINENS	☛ *Bath and Bedding*
REAL GOODS TRADING CORPORATION	☛ *Unconventional Items*
THE SEVENTH GENERATION CATALOG	☛ *Bath and Bedding*
WILLIAM GLEN	☛ *Fine China and Crystal*

WILLIAMS-SONOMA
100 North Point Street   (415) 421-7900
(corporate headquarters)
San Francisco, CA 94133

🚶 🖥 ⬚

Williams-Sonoma wants to make registering at one of its stores an extremely personal experience. To that end, you must set up a one-on-one consultation with the store's registry expert. This consultation will probably occur before the store opens its doors to the public, giving you a relaxed atmosphere in which to select your gifts. Upon arrival, you'll be given a beautifully printed gift registry booklet with detailed information on items available in the store along with a form you can fill out as you walk around.

Popular registry items include Krups espresso makers, Calphalon professional nonstick cookware, and KitchenAid standing mixers. You can also register for soufflé dishes, ice-cream makers, and dish towels. Williams-Sonoma often carries seasonal items, so before adding something to your list, be sure to find out whether it will be available at the time your guests will be shopping for gifts.

Williams-Sonoma promises to enter all your selections into its central computer within 24 hours of your consultation and have your registry list available for guests to access the very next business day. A week later, a copy of your registry list will be mailed to you. This is an excellent opportunity to make sure all the information on your registry is correct.

Unfortunately, the computer that holds all the registry information is completely separate from Williams-Sonoma's mail-order division, and guests cannot access your registry by calling the catalog. However, if a guest doesn't live near a store (which is pretty unlikely since there are 110 stores nationwide, nearly 30 in California alone), any Williams-Sonoma store will gladly describe your registry over the phone or mail a copy of the list to the gift giver. Then, that guest can purchase an item over the phone with a credit card and have the gift delivered via UPS standard delivery. Williams-Sonoma keeps a record of who buys you what, so if a gift is delivered to your home and it is unclear who the sender is, it will be able to track down the purchaser for you.

The store updates your list with every purchase made. However, if your guests who visit a store to buy your gift don't let the cashier know they are purchasing a gift from your list, then Williams-Sonoma won't be able to prevent your receiving duplications.

Because Williams-Sonoma doesn't have any sort of store locator service, it provides each couple who registers there with a list of its store locations. Most couples send this list to their parents to help guide guests to the store nearest them. Williams-Sonoma will also give you up to 50 registry cards so you can let guests know you've registered there.

Store hours vary by location.

YIELD HOUSE ☞ *Home Decor*

ZONA
97 Greene Street (212) 925-6750
New York, NY 10012 (800) 844-4790
🚶 🎞️

The flagship Zona store, encompassing 4,000 square feet in Manhattan's trendy SoHo neighborhood, has quite an eclectic mix of merchandise. There are staid items, such as French bath soaps, flannel sheets, handmade armoires, wall units, and shelves. In addition, you'll find psychedelic rock posters from the 1960s, handcrafted wrought iron chandeliers, and a 1920s vintage corkscrew collection from England and Italy. However, what catches the attention of most brides and grooms is Zona's wonderful selection of dinnerware.

There's Cassis Tabletop from France. This handmade line of ceramic dishes, bowls, and cups from Provence are of a simple design but are painted in such shocking colors as cobalt blue and mustard yellow. They're bound to make any dinner party a colorful event. (There are also toned-down versions in more earthy colors.) Tabellini flatware from Italy is created from aged Italian pewter, and Peggy Potter bowls, by a Vermont artist of the same name, are made from wood and handpainted. Couples tend to go for the small, medium, and large salad bowls.

Zona has five locations around the world.

Besides the SoHo store, there's one in East Hampton, New York; Aspen; Firenze, Italy; and Tokyo, Japan. Most people register at—and most of their guests shop at—the three U.S. locations.

When you register in person you can wander the store alone, writing down your selections, or you can have a sales associate work with you. Unless you request it, your wish list won't be sent to any other Zona location. So if your guests might shop in a Zona other than the one where you registered, you'll need to speak up.

Luckily, your guests don't have to get to a store to shop for your gift. They can also use Zona's toll-free number, (800) 844-4790, to make purchases over the phone. Each time a purchase is made, Zona marks down the purchaser's name. In case you need help later with writing thank-you notes because you can't remember who gave you what, you'll be able to turn to the store for assistance.

You and your guests can call (800) 844-4790 daily from 10:00 A.M. to 6:00 P.M. eastern time. Most Zona stores are open Monday through Saturday from 11:30 A.M. to 6:00 P.M. and Sunday from 12:00 noon to 6:00 P.M. local time.

Appendix: Registry Checklist

Where We Registered	Item	Quantity	Date Received	Received From	Thank-You Note (Y/N)	Date Note Sent

Index of Stores in Alphabetical Order

Before you picked up this book, you and your fiancé may have had a vague idea of some of the places you'd like to register. So that you'll have an easy time determining whether or not those stores are included in this book, here's an alphabetical listing of all the stores, catalogs, and companies that *The Bridal Registry Book* covers.

Index of Stores in Geographical Order

For many couples, it makes the most sense to register at a store that is located nearby—especially if they intend to register in person. The following geographical listing should help you find businesses located nearest to you.

Please note: Many department stores included in this book are owned by companies that have more than one department store, such as Federated, which owns Macy's and Bullock's. In the states where these companies have more than one department store, you'll find a combined listing. (For example, because California has both Macy's and Bullock's stores, the California listing appears as "Macy's/Bullock's.") However, when a state has only one of the stores, that store name appears in the listing. (Under the New York heading, for instance, only the name Macy's appears, because there are no Bullock's stores there.)

Also of note: Catalogs and stores that require you to utilize a mail-order division are listed under the state where that mail-order division is located. For example, even though Tower Records has stores nationwide, you must register through its New York–based mail-order office. Thus, Tower Records appears under the New York heading.

COLORADO

INDIANA

WYOMING

Index of Stores in Subject Order

This index reflects the order of store listings as they appear in this book and will help you determine which stores carry what kinds of merchandise. For example, if you know you only want to register for kitchen accessories, check out the stores listed here under Whole Kitchen Kaboodle. Then flip to the pages in that section of the book and read detailed listings of store offerings. Because many stores stock merchandise in more than one category, they are cross-referenced in the book and are marked as such here with an asterisk.

DEPARTMENT STORES

BATH & BEDDING

FINE CHINA AND CRYSTAL

HOME DECOR

HOME IMPROVEMENT

HONEYMOON

SPORTING GOODS

UNCONVENTIONAL ITEMS

THE WHOLE KITCHEN KABOODLE

Letter from the Author

The premise of *The Bridal Registry Book* was to give engaged couples a comprehensive registry source. In researching this book, I did the best I could to find the best registry programs out there. However, it is likely that after the book goes to print, more stores will begin offering registry programs, many of which may be notable and worthy of inclusion in a future edition of the book. If you know of any such stores, please write me. If you or someone you know registered at one of these establishments, be sure to let me know what the experience was like. Please include the store's full name, address, and phone number.

In addition, I'd also like to hear from readers who took my advice and registered at a store or stores listed in the book. Please keep in touch with me and describe how the registry process went. For example, was the service you and your guests received what you expected, better than expected, or, unfortunately, less than what you expected? Were the bridal consultants helpful? Were you pleased with the selection of items? Please feel free to include anything else that you might want to share with me.

Thank you very much for buying and using this book. I look forward to hearing from you.

Leah Ingram

Please send all correspondence to

Leah Ingram
P.O. Box 130273
Ann Arbor, Michigan 48113-0273